OECD Study on the World Organisation for Animal Health (OIE) Observatory

STRENGTHENING THE IMPLEMENTATION OF INTERNATIONAL STANDARDS

OECD

BETTER POLICIES FOR BETTER LIVES

Please cite this publication as:
OECD (2020), *OECD Study on the World Organisation for Animal Health (OIE) Observatory: Strengthening the Implementation of International Standards*, OECD Publishing, Paris, *https://doi.org/10.1787/c88edbcd-en*.

ISBN 978-92-64-88181-5 (print)
ISBN 978-92-64-35310-7 (pdf)

Preface

The World Organisation for Animal Health's (OIE) mission is to foster global co-operation to improve animal health, animal welfare and veterinary public health worldwide. OIE Members develop and adopt international standards to better co-ordinate their approach to prevent and control animal diseases, facilitate safe international trade as well as strengthen national Veterinary Services.

Our Members face a growing challenge to co-ordinate their policy making to manage global sanitary risks in a world which is becoming increasingly globalised and complex. Indeed, animal diseases and zoonoses know no borders, as demonstrated by the ongoing transboundary spread of foot and mouth disease, avian influenza and African swine fever, among many other examples.

We know that many OIE Members face challenges in the implementation of our international standards. Understanding to what extent and how the OIE standards are used by Members is essential to ensure our standards are fit for purpose and relevant. In May 2018, the World Assembly of OIE Delegates adopted a resolution recommending that an Observatory on the implementation of OIE standards be established to address these issues.

For such an ambitious and challenging project, the OIE entered into a specific collaboration with the Organisation for Economic Co-operation and Development (OECD) to explore the potential solutions for the design of the OIE Observatory. Using its expertise in international regulatory cooperation, the OECD carried out the study reported in this document which provides an analysis of key features of OIE standards, as well as a review of the existing sources of information in relation to their implementation.

The OECD study highlights that a project to monitor implementation of OIE standards will be complex and challenging because of the voluntary nature of the OIE standards, and the variability of implementing mechanisms. We know that OIE Members use a range of approaches in implementing OIE standards because of differences in sanitary situations, legal frameworks and procedures, public and private sector relationships, national systems for production and processing, trade profiles and acceptable levels of risks.

Despite this complexity, the OECD has provided recommendations to assist the OIE in the design of the OIE Observatory. The OIE Observatory is an important strategic and long-term project for the OIE, that will contribute to the strengthening of international harmonisation of national sanitary measures.

I would finally like to emphasise that this study was developed in the framework of OECD work on international regulatory co-operation and the partnership of international organisation for effective international rulemaking, to which the OIE is actively contributing along with 50 other international organisations. Learning collectively from the experiences of international organisations helps us to understand how international organisations can promote multilateral solutions and improve our collective contribution to a sustainable future.

Monique Eloit
OIE Director General

Foreword

The protection of animal health and welfare is one of many areas where governments can benefit from co-operating internationally and co-ordinating their national policies. Without the implementation of prevention and control measures, animal diseases can spread both within and between countries. The dissemination of animal diseases around the world can be devastating for animal production, human health (for zoonotic diseases) and have serious consequences for national economies. Intergovernmental co-operation is therefore essential to prevent the spread of diseases across borders and to provide sanitary measures that ensure safe international trade of live animals and animal products.

The World Organisation for Animal Health (OIE) is an international organisation developing and adopting international standards that if implemented safeguard animal health worldwide. In order to monitor the implementation of these common standards across countries, the OIE has decided to establish an Observatory. It is an ambitious project that has great potential to gather tangible information on the use of OIE standards in countries.

Based on an in-depth analysis of the OIE and its normative work, this study finds that OIE standards are a reference in the areas of animal health, animal welfare and zoonoses. Many data collection mechanisms already provide information about the implementation of OIE standards. However, monitoring of implementation of these standards is not yet systematic, and information remains limited in scope and irregular in frequency. This study provides recommendations on how the OIE can use its existing institutional framework and information-collection mechanisms to support the OIE Observatory.

The study builds on OECD long-standing work on regulatory policy and governance, as set out in the *OECD 2012 Recommendation of the Council on Regulatory Policy and Governance*. It was developed in the framework of OECD work on international regulatory co-operation (IRC) (Principle 12 of the Recommendation), within the Partnership of International Organisations for Effective International Rulemaking (IO Partnership). It is part of a series started in 2014 that provides detailed overviews of the structure, governance, instruments and processes of international organisations (IOs) in support of international rule-making and standard-setting.

To date, the series includes the cases of the OECD, the International Maritime Organization (IMO), the Food and Agriculture Organization of the United Nations (FAO), the International Organization for Standardization (ISO), the International Organization of Legal Metrology (OIML), the World Health Organization (WHO), the UN Economic Commission for Europe (UNECE), the World Trade Organization (WTO) and the Bureau International des Poids et Mesures (BIPM). The case studies complement broader analytical work conducted by the IO partnership that compares the governance modalities and rule-making processes of 50 IOs, annual meetings and technical discussions within five working groups.

The work on international regulatory co-operation by IOs is conducted under the auspices of the OECD Regulatory Policy Committee, whose mandate is to assist both members and non-members in building and strengthening capacity for regulatory quality and regulatory reform.

This report was approved by the OECD Regulatory Policy Committee by written procedure on 30 September 2019 and prepared for publication by the OECD Secretariat.

Acknowledgements

This study was prepared by the OECD Public Governance Directorate under the leadership of Marcos Bonturi, Director. It was co-ordinated and drafted by Céline Kauffmann and Marianna Karttunen from the OECD Regulatory Policy Division under the overall direction of Nick Malyshev, Head of the Regulatory Policy Division. This study was developed with significant inputs from OIE staff and OIE Member Countries, OECD Members and other international organisations. This work was funded by the OIE thanks to contributions received from the Government of the United Kingdom of Great Britain and Northern Ireland. The study was circulated for comments to the Regulatory Policy Committee in April and November 2019, and to the IO partnership in April 2019. The authors are also grateful for the reading done by the Editorial Board of the OECD Public Governance Directorate, including Eva Beuselinck, Klas Klaas and Andrea Uhrhammer. The study was prepared for publication by Jennifer Stein, with administrative assistance provided by Claudia Paupe.

The authors wish to thank OIE staff and Member countries for responses to interviews and several rounds of comments. Special thanks in particular go to Director-General Monique Eloit for her vision and support throughout the project as well as to OIE Deputy Director Generals, Jean-Philippe Dop and Matthew Stone. We are very grateful to Karen Bucher, Diana Tellechea and Gillian Mylrea from the OIE Standards Department for their extensive inputs throughout the process and for facilitating the preparation of this study. The study also benefitted from inputs from staff of other international organisations, in particular the Codex Alimentarius, the European Commission, the Eurasian Economic Commission, the Food and Agriculture Organisation of the United Nations, the Gulf Co-operation Council Standardization Organization, the International Plant Protection Convention, the Standards and Trade Development Facility and the World Trade Organisation.

Table of contents

Abbreviations and acronyms   8

Executive summary   10

1 Characterisation of the body of OIE normative instruments   13
  Overview of OIE normative instruments, focus on explanation of OIE Codes and Manuals   15
  OIE organisational structure supporting its normative activity   18
  Implementation of OIE normative instruments   21
  Conclusion: Key features of the body of OIE normative instruments   27
  Notes   28
  References   30

2 Existing mechanisms supporting and monitoring the implementation of OIE
  standards   31
  Mechanisms collecting information on countries' animal health and welfare system: the PVS
  Pathway   33
  Mechanisms to collect information on the sanitary status of OIE listed diseases for country, zone
  or compartment   39
  External WTO mechanisms to collect information on trade impacts of veterinary measures   45
  Mechanisms to collect information and support implementation of specific thematic or regional
  issues   48
  Conclusion: Key features of existing mechanisms supporting and monitoring the implementation
  of OIE standards   52
  Notes   53
  References   55

3 Recommendations for the establishment of the OIE Observatory   57
  Setting the objectives of the OIE Observatory   58
  Defining the scope of the OIE Observatory   61
  Highlighting some key principles of how the Observatory will operate   66
  Notes   68
  References   69

Tables

Figures

Boxes

Abbreviations and acronyms

AHS	African horse sickness
AMR	Anti-microbial resistance
AMU	Anti-microbial use
ASTM	American Society for Testing and Materials
BSE	Bovine spongiform encephalopathy
CBPP	Contagious bovine pleuropneumonia
CSF	Classical swine fever
DSD	Disease Status Department
FAO	Food and Agriculture Organization
FMD	Foot and mouth disease
HPAI	High pathogenic avian influenza
IEC	International Electrotechnical Commission
IHR	International Health Regulations
ILO	International Labour Organisation
IOs	International organisations
IPPC	International Plant Protection Convention
IRSS	Implementation Review and Support System
ISO	International Organization for Standardization
ISPMs	International Standards for Phytosanitary Measures
MoUs	Memoranda of Understanding
OIE	World Organisation for Animal Health (*Organisation mondiale de la santé animale*)
PPR	Peste des petits ruminants

PRRS	Porcine reproductive and respiratory syndrome
PVS	Performance of Veterinary Services
SCAD	Scientific Commission for Animal Diseases
STCs	Specific Trade Concerns
SPS	Sanitary and Phytosanitary Measures
TPRM	Trade Policy Review Mechanism
VLIM	Veterinary legislation identification missions
VLSP	Veterinary Legislation Support Programme
WAD	World Assembly of Delegates
WAHIAD	World Animal Health Information and Analysis Department
WAHIS	World Animal Health Information System
WTO	World Trade Organization

Executive summary

This study provides a diagnostic of the existing normative work, related governance structure and information collection mechanisms of the World Organisation for Animal Health (OIE) and provides recommendations to support the OIE in establishing an Observatory on the Implementation of Standards.

The OIE is the intergovernmental organisation responsible for animal health worldwide. It develops a corpus of different voluntary normative instruments, commonly referred to as OIE international standards, which aim to ensure transparency around animal health status, build good governance of veterinary services and support safe trade of animals and animal products. These OIE standards – and particularly the Codes and Manuals that are the core normative instruments of the OIE – are recognised as the reference standards in the areas of animal health, animal welfare and zoonoses, putting the organisation in a good position to identify and monitor their impacts. Domestically, veterinary authorities recognise the usefulness of OIE standards in developing national measures for improving animal health, animal welfare and international trade, and confirm consulting the OIE Codes and Manuals regularly in this regard. OIE Codes and Manuals are developed following a largely expert-driven and participatory standard-setting procedure, resulting in cutting-edge reference standards.

Despite their recognised usefulness by OIE Members, evidence on the actual uptake of OIE standards in domestic legislation remains scarce. This does not necessarily mean these standards are not used; indeed, OIE Members confirm a strong demand for them. Rather, it reflects an uneven process for the domestic application of OIE standards and inconsistent monitoring of their use. Given the voluntary nature of OIE standards, the implementation process is neither defined nor prescribed by the OIE. Members have much leeway in considering, referencing and using OIE standards. This results in varied approaches across OIE Members, making it difficult to measure the consistency of national measures with OIE standards.

This study identifies 13 data collection mechanisms at international or regional level that are used, or may be used, to gather information on the implementation of OIE standards in domestic jurisdictions. While most of these mechanisms are set up by the OIE itself, others exist in the context of the WTO, or of the European Union for example. Initially, these mechanisms were developed to address specific needs, such as providing transparency on disease status, evaluating the quality and building domestic capacity of veterinary services, or monitoring the effects of domestic regulations on international trade. As a result, they are focussed primarily on fulfilling these specific needs rather than gathering systematic evidence on the implementation of OIE standards. The information obtained through these processes is therefore limited in scope and irregular in frequency, and does not necessarily assess the link with the use of OIE individual standards.

Overall, a disconnect remains between the process of implementation by OIE Members and the standard-setting process at the OIE level, as is often the case across international organisations. The views of Members on the uses made of OIE standards are not systematically gathered and shared with the OIE Secretariat or other Members. Better information on implementation could be used to improve new or revised standards developed by the OIE and ensure their continued relevance over time for veterinary authorities across OIE Members. The information would also help to better prioritise and target capacity-building activities and refine the understanding of good practices in the implementation of OIE standards. This report identifies opportunities for gathering such information in a more systematic manner, and supports the establishment by the OIE of an Observatory on the implementation of its standards.

The OIE Observatory is an ambitious project largely unprecedented among IOs. Based on the diagnostic of the current state of play in the OIE, the OECD study provides recommendations related to the objectives of the Observatory, the definition of its scope, and its operational modalities as described below. These build on the broad range of relevant IO experiences as reflected in the IO Partnership, and have been tailored to the OIE standards and governance structure.

Key recommendations

Setting the objectives of the Observatory

Given the nature of OIE standards and existing data collection mechanisms, the Observatory should focus on two complementary objectives:

- Identifying Members' capacity development needs and successful practices in implementing OIE standards
- Enhancing the standard-setting process through evidence-based assessment of the actual use of OIE standards.

Defining the scope of the Observatory

- Continue to map the OIE standards that are already the object of data collection. This involves identifying the following aspects of the existing collection mechanisms: the connection with the underlying OIE standards; the geographic coverage; the frequency of the collected information; the nature of information; the level of availability of the information and the level of the validation of the information.
- Start by focusing on the implementation of OIE standards (mostly from the Terrestrial and Aquatic Codes) that already benefit from data coverage.
- As the Observatory consolidates its working methods, data collection and analytical capacity, and establishes its credibility, gradually expand the scope of OIE standards included.
- Continue analysing Members' practices in implementing OIE standards and their contribution to achieving the organisation's objectives.
- Systematise, standardise and expand existing sources of information.
- Co-operate with FAO, WTO, EU to make better use of their data and cross check information collected by the OIE.

Deciding the operational modalities

- Define the key outputs of the Observatory, including the level and detail of information, its availability in a user-friendly database and in analytical reports.
- Endow the Observatory with adequate resources.
- Locate the Observatory strategically to ensure that it delivers on its key objectives – by benefitting from strong connection with the information sources and the standard-setting process, as well as autonomy to carry out relevant analysis.
- Highlight transparency as a key underlying principle of the Observatory's activities.

- Establish mechanisms to benefit from stakeholder inputs and contributions, including academia, other international organisations, experts and civil society.
- Define the role of Members.

1 Characterisation of the body of OIE normative instruments

This chapter maps the corpus of normative instruments developed by the OIE, outlines the organisational structure supporting its normative activity, and describes the process of implementation of OIE standards. It finds that the OIE develops different voluntary normative instruments, commonly referred to as OIE international standards, which are recognised as reference standards in the areas of animal health (including zoonoses) and animal welfare. The Codes and Manuals, which are the core normative instruments of the OIE, are developed following a largely expert-driven and participatory standard-setting procedure. However, despite their recognised usefulness by OIE Members, evidence on the actual uptake of OIE standards in domestic legislation remains scarce, reflecting uneven process for their domestic application and inconsistent monitoring of their use. The implementation process is neither defined nor prescribed by the OIE, and Members have much leeway in considering, referencing and using OIE standards.

The OIE aims to ensure the improvement of animal health and welfare, and veterinary public health worldwide, strives to prevent the spread of diseases, and inspire trust in veterinary services. To do so, the OIE provides a comprehensive framework to support Members to achieve three interrelated objectives:

- to establish transparency on the sanitary status of animal diseases for country, zone or compartment;
- to build good governance of the national animal health and welfare systems through improved legal frameworks and resources of veterinary services;
- to support world trade in animals and animal products by ensuring safety, while avoiding unjustified sanitary barriers.[1]

To achieve its objectives, the OIE adopts a number of voluntary normative instruments for use by its Members, commonly referred to as OIE's international standards (Box 1).[2] The purpose of the OIE's international standards is to improve the health and welfare of animals throughout the world, regardless of socio-economic, religious or cultural context.

Box 1. What is an international standard?

(OECD, 2019[1]) highlights the wide range of instruments with external normative value adopted by international organisations, most of which non-legally binding. Among them, "international technical standards are voluntary instruments developed in response to a need in a particular area expressed by stakeholders through a bottom-up approach" (OECD, 2016[2]). They may be incorporated by states within their domestic legislation and/or directly implemented by private actors, which perceive their quality and relevance.

There is no recognised definition of international standards. Nevertheless, the Agreement on the Application of Sanitary and Phytosanitary Measures (SPS) of the World Trade Organization (WTO) bases their qualification on whether they come from three international bodies, including the World Organisation for Animal Health in relation to international standards for "animal health and zoonoses" (OECD/WTO, 2019[3]).

Source: (OECD, 2016[2]), International Regulatory Co-operation: The Role of International Organisations in Fostering Better Rules of Globalisation, Paris, https://dx.doi.org/10.1787/9789264244047-en; (OECD, 2019[1]), "The Contribution of International Organisations to a Rule-Based International System", Paris, www.oecd.org/gov/regulatory-policy/IO-Rule-Based%20System.pdf; (OECD/WTO, 2019[3]), Facilitating Trade Through Regulatory Co-operation: The Case of the WTO's TBT/SPS Agreements and Committees, Paris, Geneva, https://doi.org/10.1787/ad3c655f-en.

The OIE adopts five different kinds of voluntary normative instruments for use by OIE Members (Figure 1.1):

- Codes (*Terrestrial Animal Health Code*, or *Terrestrial Code*, and the *Aquatic Animal Health Code*, or *Aquatic Code*);[3]
- Manuals (*Manual of Diagnostic Tests and Vaccines for Terrestrial Animals*, or *Terrestrial Manual* and the *Manual of Diagnostic Tests for Aquatic Animals*, or *Aquatic Manual*);[4]
- Technical resolutions;
- Recommendations;
- Guidelines.

There is a specific use case of "technical resolutions" by which the OIE issues official recognition of disease status of countries for terrestrial diseases and the list of antimicrobial agents. They can both be considered as normative statements by the organisation and the outcomes of implementation of relevant sections of the OIE *Terrestrial Code* (hence their short description below and further development in the Chapter on *Existing mechanisms supporting and monitoring the implementation of OIE standards*).

The organisational setting of the OIE (Figure 1.2) is structured in a manner to ensure a high level of scientific evidence-base and regional representativeness in the development of these normative instruments, as well as follow-up support at the regional and country level in the implementation of the instruments. The "World Assembly of Delegates" is the highest authority of the OIE that meets for its General Session every year in May.[5] The OIE has a Secretariat headquartered in Paris, France, as well as regional offices, tasked with the administrative management of the organisation and in charge to support the work of the experts.

Finally, the implementation of OIE normative instruments (Figure 1.3) pertains to OIE Members. Nevertheless, the OIE provides some guidance and indications on the possible forms of implementation of OIE standards at the domestic level.

Overview of OIE normative instruments, focus on explanation of OIE Codes and Manuals

Figure 1.1 gives an overview of the OIE normative instruments that apply to OIE Members and the dynamics between them. Overall, the "core" standards developed by the OIE are the Codes and Manuals. Updates to these Codes and Manuals are adopted by Resolutions of the OIE World Assembly. In addition, for specific purposes, the Codes and Manuals are complemented by:

- Technical resolutions for official recognition of disease status and for endorsement of national official control programmes or Technical resolution on list of antimicrobial agents of veterinary importance;
- Technical resolutions adopted by the World Assembly following the presentation of technical items during General Sessions;
- Recommendations of Regional Commissions, submitted to the World Assembly for approval;
- Recommendations of Global Conferences, which may be presented to the World Assembly for information but not for endorsement;
- Guidelines developed by specialists and published on the OIE website.

Figure 1.1. Overview of OIE normative instruments

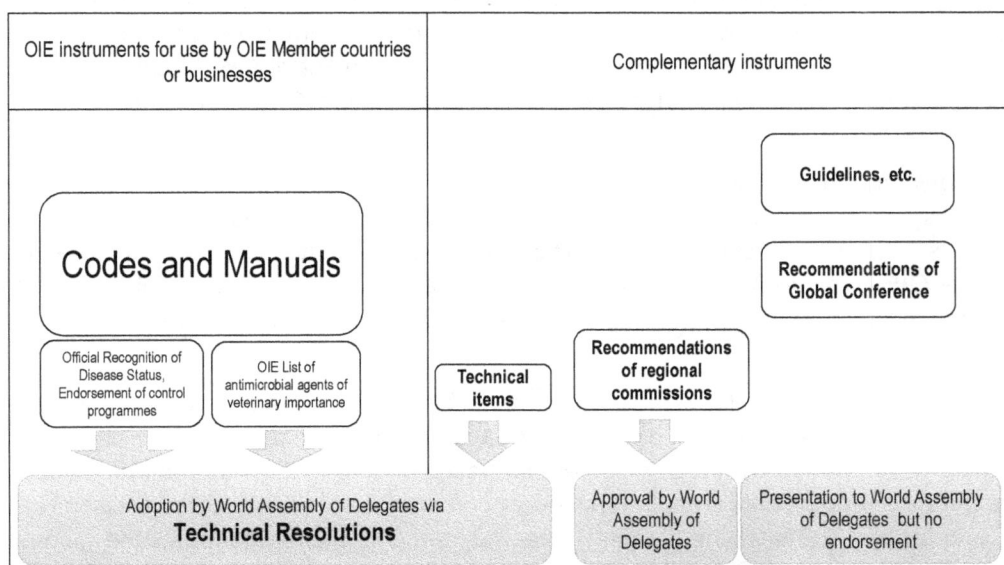

Notes: This figure focuses on instruments directed at OIE Members. It does not picture the OIE instruments that are internal administrative documents.
Source: Author's own elaboration based on OIE responses to OECD 2018 survey to international organisations.

The core of OIE instruments: Codes and Manuals

The Codes and Manuals represent the largest volume of normative work of the Organisation, are applicable to all OIE Members, and are the only ones that are subject to monitoring of implementation.

The *Terrestrial* and *Aquatic Code*s set principles to ensure the quality of veterinary services/aquatic animal health services, definitions of diseases, as well as the conditions to confirm that diseases are absent. In particular, they compile a number of international standards that contain "science-based recommendations for disease reporting, prevention and control and for assuring safe international trade in terrestrial animals (mammals, reptiles, birds and bees) and aquatic animals (amphibians, crustaceans, fish and molluscs) and their products" (OIE, 2016[4]). The OIE Codes are structured between horizontal chapters with general provisions dealing with veterinary systems and disease-specific chapters.

OIE Manuals apply to diagnostic laboratories and vaccine production, and aim to provide a uniform approach to the detection of diseases listed in the Codes. They set standards on the management of veterinary diagnostic laboratories and vaccine facilities and on the methods for validation of diagnostic tests and for the manufacture of vaccines. In addition, the main part of the *Terrestrial Manual* sets standards for diagnostic tests and vaccines mainly for specific diseases listed in the Codes as having potential for very serious and rapid spread, irrespective of national borders.[6] They therefore apply to a specific set of activities and are of use for a more limited number of domestic authorities, most directly to the laboratories carrying out veterinary diagnostic tests and surveillance and vaccine manufacturers and users.

The structures and contents of the Codes and Manuals respectively are similar for both Terrestrial and Aquatic animals, with differences mainly related to the subject matter.

OIE normative instruments complementing Codes and Manuals

In complement to the Codes and Manuals, the OIE also adopts other instruments: namely resolutions, recommendations or guidelines. Overall, their objective is to complement the Codes and Manuals with more specific guidance either applicable to a regional context or to a specific thematic need.

Technical resolutions are the normative instrument of the World Assembly of Delegates that serve as a formal adoption by the entire Membership of documents developed by Specialist Commissions, or by the OIE in specific contexts. In particular, technical resolutions serve to formally adopt: technical items of the WAD (World Assembly of Delegates), developed by the OIE; the list of OIE Members and zones with disease-free status officially recognised by the OIE; as well as the OIE list of antimicrobial agents of veterinary importance.

Recommendations may be adopted either at the regional or at the global level. At the regional level, recommendations are developed by the Regional Commissions, on issues relevant to their respective regional interests. The recommendations are discussed and elaborated during a Regional Conference convened by the OIE Director-General every two years. The recommendations are then integrated into a report of the Regional Commission submitted to the General Session of the "World Assembly of Delegates" for approval.[7]

At the global level, recommendations may be adopted by the participants (that may include Member countries, experts, donors, etc.) of a Global Conference, organised on a specific topic on an ad hoc basis. Recommendations are drafted by the OIE Secretariat based on information shared and discussed during the global conference. Participants are left with time for comments, during dedicated sessions in the Global conference, and for a period after the meeting. After this, the OIE Secretariat posts the recommendation to its website. The recommendations of the Global Conferences are shared with the World Assembly of Delegates in May, for information, not for endorsement.

Guidelines are developed by the specialists designated by the OIE secretariat and published on the OIE website without following a systematic pre-established procedure. They are not endorsed by the World Assembly of Delegates. They are developed to provide guidance on a specific topic, often in complement of existing standards in the OIE Codes or Manuals. The name of such documents may vary, namely guidelines, checklists or tools.

As an example of such documents, the Checklist on the Practical Application of Compartmentalisation supports veterinary authorities and private sector in interpreting and complying with OIE standards from the *Terrestrial Code,* which establishes the principle of compartmentalisation. It therefore sets six broad principles that go from the definition of a compartment the separation of a compartment from potential sources of infection, and surveillance for the agent or disease, to emergency responses and notifications as well as supervision and control of compartments. Other examples of guidelines include the Guidelines for Animal Disease Control (OIE, 2014[5]), the Guidelines for Investigation of Suspicious Biological Events (OIE, 2018[6]) and the Guidelines on the Veterinary Education Core Curriculum (OIE, 2013[7]). The PVS Tool for the Evaluation of Performance of Veterinary Services (OIE, 2019[8]), although not formally classified as such, operates and has similar status to OIE guidelines.

In addition to these instruments which apply to OIE Members, the OIE also adopts instruments that are rather directed at the OIE Secretariat, for administrative purposes (e.g. administrative resolutions), for staff and organisational purposes (Codes of conduct), or for setting co-operation objectives with other international bodies (Memoranda of Understanding, MoUs). These MoUs are not so much normative instruments directed at OIE Members, but rather agreements with other international organisations or non-governmental organisations.[8] Resolutions may be adopted for internal administrative purposes or with an effect for all OIE Members.

Sui generis *OIE normative instrument: Official Recognition of Disease Status and the OIE List of antimicrobial agents*

In addition to these families of instruments, the OIE develops two forms of sui generis normative instruments, on the basis of provisions of the Codes and Manuals, formally adopted by technical resolutions of the General Assembly. This is the case for Official Recognition of Disease Status and of the OIE List of antimicrobial agents of veterinary importance.

The "Official Recognition of Disease Status" issued by the OIE, and the related endorsement of national official control programmes, provides a unique form of normative instrument in support of the implementation of the OIE *Terrestrial Code* and *Manual.* Following an in-depth procedure to verify the compliance of OIE Members' with certain standards of the *Terrestrial Code* and *Manual* (described further below), the Official Recognition of Disease Status results in a normative document adopted by the World Assembly of Delegates via a technical resolution (see Box 3.3). The Official Recognition of Disease Status thus serves both as a statement of compliance with OIE *Terrestrial Code* and *Manual* and as a standalone normative document in itself.

The OIE List of antimicrobial agents of veterinary importance was first established by the OIE, following a call by an expert workshop on Non-Human Antimicrobial Usage and Antimicrobial Resistance between the FAO/OIE/WHO in 2003. It is a normative document serving as a reference on all antimicrobials that are important in veterinary medicine. The list was initially developed by an ad hoc group on antimicrobial resistance, followed by a survey questionnaire sent by the OIE Director General to all OIE Members. It is regularly updated – the latest update took place in May 2018 (OIE, 2018[9]).

OIE organisational structure supporting its normative activity

Given the highly technical nature of the OIE mandate and normative activity, the OIE governance structure reflects an expert-driven organisation. A substantive part of OIE normative activity is carried out by several groups bringing together experts from Member countries to continuously monitor the evolutions of scientific information on epidemiology and ensuring a science-based standard-setting process. In addition, similarly to other intergovernmental organisations, the OIE provides several platforms for its Members to meet regularly, both to provide strategic leadership (World Assembly of Delegates; Council), as well as to ensure close contact with regional specificities (Regional Commissions). The OIE Secretariat provides institutional support to OIE Members in these different groups. Figure 1.2 describes these three different types of organs.

The expert-driven nature of the OIE is particularly apparent throughout the standard-setting procedure of the OIE Codes and Manuals, which go through a thorough multi-layered process between experts and OIE Members. This confirms the highly technical nature of OIE Codes and Manuals, as well as their significance in the overall body of instruments of the OIE.

Figure 1.2. Organs involved in the conduct of OIE work

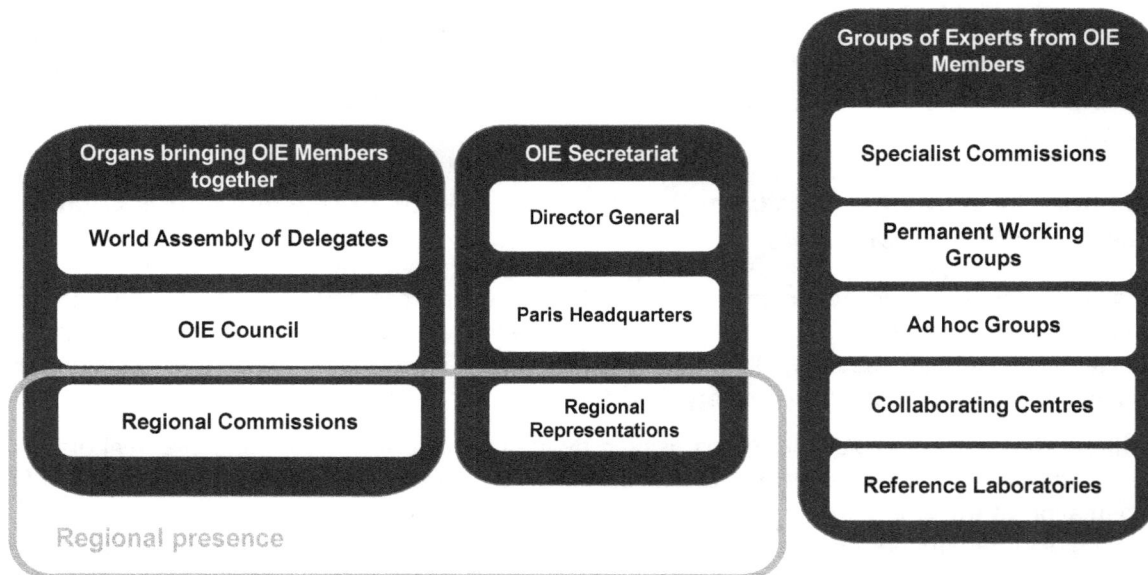

Notes: Author's own elaboration. This figure describes the existing organs involved in the conduct of OIE work. It does not prejudge any hierarchy between the organs.
Source: www.oie.int/about-us/wo/.

Overview of OIE organisational structure

The OIE is structured around direct representations of OIE Members, giving the strategic leadership to the organisation; groups of experts, conducting the core of the standard-setting work of the organisation; as well as the OIE Secretariat, supporting the Members and experts. Specific representations of the Organisation is provided at the regional level to ensure the inclusiveness of the OIE work with all OIE Members.

The OIE is led by a World Assembly of Delegates (WAD) bringing together delegates from veterinary authorities of all OIE Member countries once a year in May. The WAD has the authority to review and endorse normative instruments, and in particular Codes and Manuals. The WAD is supported by the

Council, composed by a sub-set of nine elected Members from OIE Member countries, representing all regions and meeting at least twice a year in Paris.[9]

Under the leadership of these organs, which represent the entire Membership, the core of the organisation's standard-setting is conducted by different specialised groups of experts, ensuring that the different normative instruments are state of the art and evidence-based. Specialist Commissions are namely the bodies that have oversight over the standard-setting process. There are four Specialist commissions[10] that meet on a regular basis, and may propose to the OIE Director-General to convene an ad hoc group or one of the permanent working groups[11] for the development of certain standards, as described in Figure 1.4.

Collaborating Centres and Reference Laboratories allow to provide expert support to OIE Members on specific topics. The Collaborating Centres are networks of experts set up to provide expertise on specific topics of competence in some cases for particular regions,[12] and may be solicited when experts are needed, for example for constituting ad hoc groups. The Reference Laboratories provide scientific and technical advice on diagnosis and control of specific diseases.[13]

In addition, a number of regional groups are set up to ensure that the interests and needs of specific regions and countries are well reflected in the multilateral setting. Regional commissions meet at the regional level and reconvene their respective positions and priorities to the WAD at the annual meeting.

Finally, the everyday work of the OIE is carried out by a relatively small secretariat in comparison with other intergovernmental organisations, composed of 163 people.[14] It is nevertheless in line with other standard-setting bodies (e.g. ASTM – 200; IEC – 110; IFAC – 79; ISO – 136) (OECD, 2016[2]). The work of this secretariat consists in supporting the various expert groups, facilitating the development and implementation of OIE standards, and more broadly, helping OIE Members ensure implementation of the Organisation's mandate and strategic plans.

The Secretariat functions under the general leadership of the Director-General, who, with the support of two Deputy Directors General and a Financial Director provides a transversal vision of the work of the organisation. It is under the responsibility of the Director-General that a five-year Strategic Plan is set, in close collaboration with the OIE Council. This Plan builds on latest scientific and governance advances and results of previous strategic plans and ensures that the OIE continues to contribute effectively to societal changes.[15]

The more technical work of the organisation is conducted by units under the authority of the two Deputy Directors General, who head two "pillars" of work (see Figure 1.3: i) institutional affairs and regional activities; and ii) international standards and science. The first pillar deals with organisational governance, communications, legal affairs, governance of the Veterinary Services (through the Performance of Veterinary Services Pathway), Member support (including capacity building) and strategic co-operation. The second pillar focuses on substantive matters, which are conducted by individual units, such as WAHIS (World Animal Health Information System), standards, status, programmes, anti-microbial resistance and veterinary products, science, and publications.

To ensure regional representativeness, the work of the headquarters is complemented by work of regional representations, involving offices of the OIE Secretariat based directly in Africa, Americas, Asia and the Pacific, Europe, Middle East.

Figure 1.3. OIE 2019 organisational chart

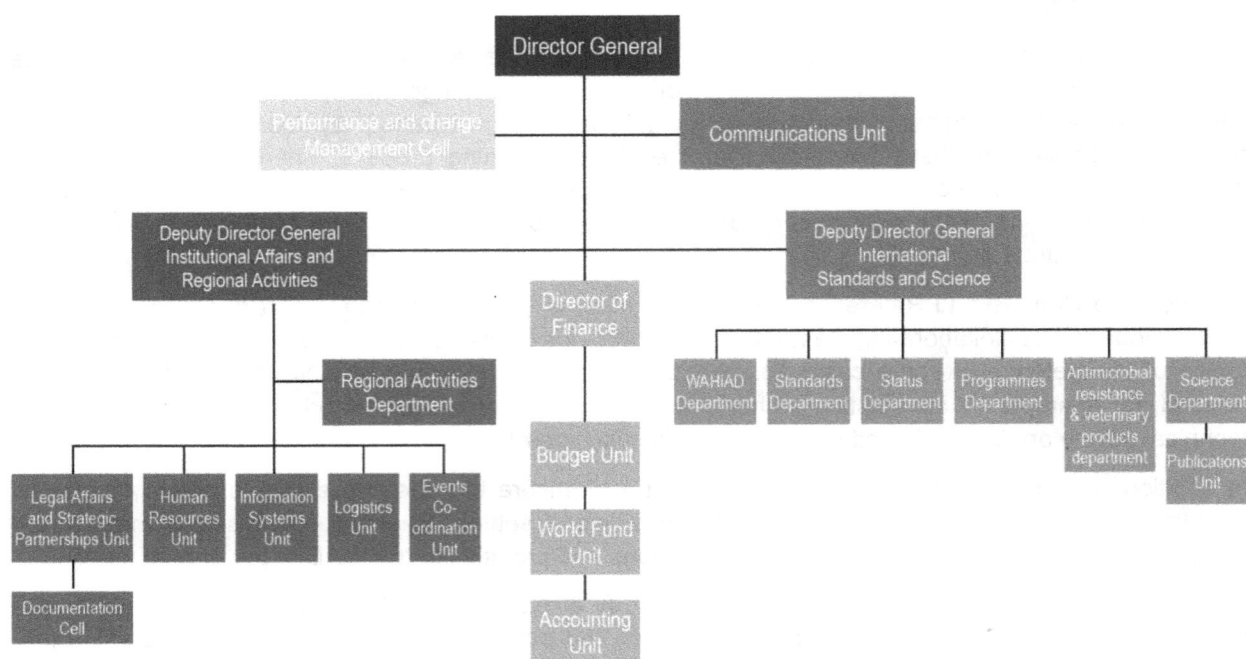

Source: Information provided by the OIE

Conduct of OIE normative activity

The standard-setting procedure for the OIE Codes and Manuals is the most rigorous and formal procedure within the OIE normative activity together with the specific procedure for the official recognition of disease status. The other normative instruments are developed on a more ad hoc basis and organically.

The Codes are developed following the procedure described in Figure 1.4. The standard-setting procedure starts with a proposal for a new or revised standard, following a topic, issue, problem identified by a Member country, a specialist commission, or an international/regional organisation with whom the OIE has an official agreement. The proposals for a new or revised standard are included in the work programmes of Specialist Commissions.[16] Depending on the specific needs of the standard, the Specialist Commissions may suggest to use the expertise of an ad hoc Group (convened at the initiative of the Director General) or of one of the permanent Working Groups of independent experts (formed by decision of the World Assembly of Delegates upon recommendation of the Director General).

At each February and September meetings, the Specialist Commissions review the drafts and share with OIE Members for comments, and review the comments (or revert back to experts as relevant). Normally, there are at least two review cycles (over two years) between Specialist commissions and permanent working groups or ad hoc groups to leave time for Members to become acquainted with the draft, comment on it, and facilitate consensus-based adoption by the World Assembly of Delegates. Once the final draft is agreed upon, the relevant specialist commission shares the draft text with all OIE Members in March, two months in advance of the World Assembly of Delegates. This leaves OIE Members two months to examine the final drafts before eventually adoption by consensus in the World Assembly of Delegates in May (OIE, 2016[4]).

This same procedure is followed for both *Terrestrial* and *Aquatic Codes*. Nevertheless, the public authorities in charge of setting aquatic and terrestrial animals may be different. The engagement of the authorities on Terrestrial and Aquatic standards is therefore not systematically the same, whether in the standard-setting process or in the implementation of standards. As a result, the engagement in the development of aquatic standards is sometimes considered less active.

In principle, Manuals follow a very similar procedure as the Codes. They are however rarely developed through ad hoc or permanent working groups in practice, but rather by Reference Laboratory experts and the Biological and Aquatic Specialist Commissions. In addition, they usually go through only one review cycle, instead of two review cycles usually followed for OIE Codes.

This procedure is specific to the OIE standards, and differs from the procedure followed to set other OIE normative instruments. In particular, Administrative decisions related to the operation of the OIE (Administrative Resolutions) are developed in consultation with the OIE Council and adopted by OIE Member countries during the World Assembly. Technical Resolutions related to the Technical items are developed with the support of the Rapporteur and voluntary Member Countries during the General Session of the World Assembly. Recommendations of Regional Commissions are developed during Regional Conferences.[17]

Figure 1.4. Yearly standard-setting procedure for OIE Codes and Manuals

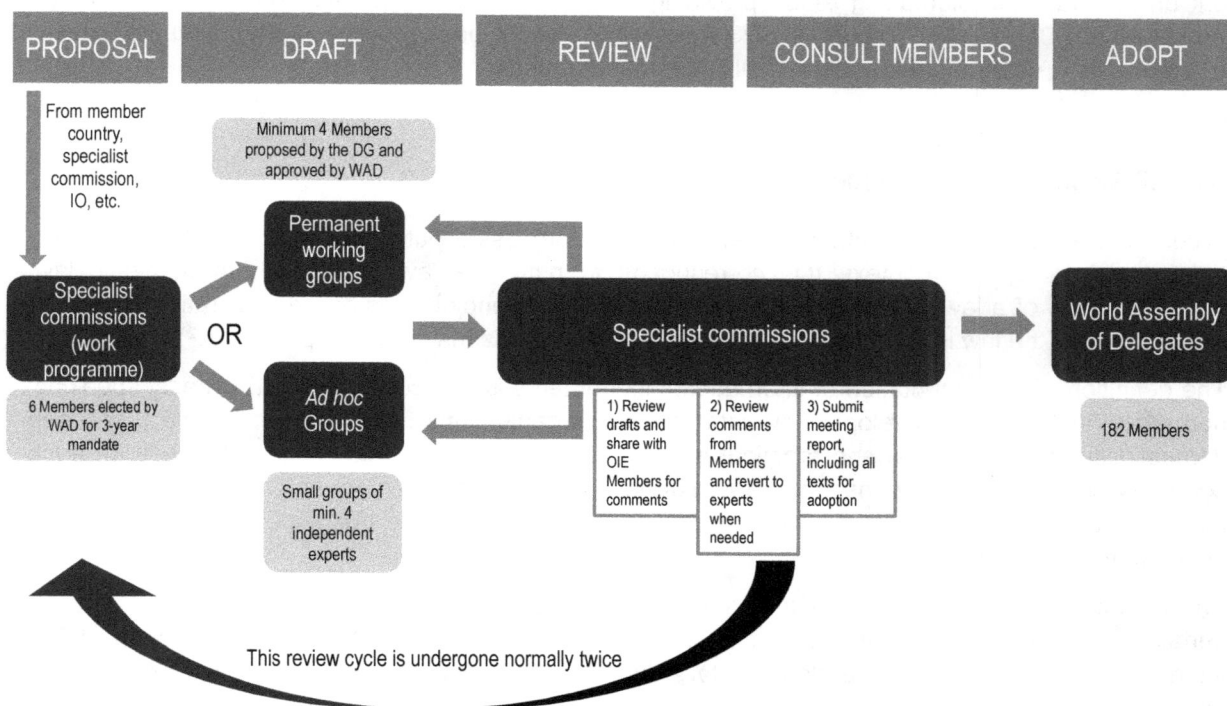

Source: Author's own elaboration based on (OIE, 2016[4]), *Procedures used by the OIE to set standards and recommendations for international trade, with a focus on the Terrestrial and aquatic animal health codes,* http://www.oie.int/fileadmin/Home/eng/Internationa_Standard_Setting/docs/pdf/A_OIE_procedures_standards_2016.pdf.

Implementation of OIE normative instruments

OIE normative instruments are voluntary for OIE Members, even though their use is strongly incentivised by the WTO SPS Agreement (see below). In OIE normative framework, the only obligation for OIE Member countries is to notify disease status and disease control measures, in virtue of the Organic Statutes of the OIE.[18] This notification obligation was later embedded in the *Terrestrial* and *Aquatic Code*s. The voluntary nature of OIE normative instruments has several consequences, namely:

- OIE Members may adopt and use the instruments in a manner that is most relevant to their specific conditions, such as their disease status, domestic regulatory framework, etc. In particular, all OIE normative instruments may not be relevant to all countries;

- OIE Members may choose a higher level of protection than those in the OIE instruments if they have a scientific justification. This is acknowledged by the WTO SPS Agreement (art. 3.3). Certain standards in the OIE Codes provide specific methodologies on risk analysis, which may help OIE Members in providing such scientific justification while respecting OIE standards.

Like for international instruments more broadly, the process for implementing OIE standards is not easily defined (Box 1.2). Neither the OIE, nor another source of international law (WTO requirements for example) define specifically a preferred path or specific modalities for their implementation, or prescribe the approach to adopt. As a result, there is a wide variation of implementation practices across OIE Members.

Still, a number of provisions of the OIE Codes and Manuals provide guiding language to support OIE Members in their efforts to implement specific technical aspects of OIE standards. This is in line with the common practice of international organisations - two thirds of IOs surveyed by the OECD as part of its work on international rulemaking report providing a description of implementation in their instruments themselves (OECD, 2019[1]). The WTO SPS Agreement also includes provisions promoting the uptake of OIE standards in veterinary legislation of OIE Member countries.

Box 1.2. Defining implementation

In common language, implementation is defined as "The process of putting a decision or plan into effect; execution".[1] In a legal context, this corresponds to putting a law into effect. In domestic law, implementation of a law typically entails that a regulatory agency issues an administrative regulation specifying how the law is going to enter into effect and how citizens must comply with it.[2]

The definition of implementation of international instruments is particularly difficult. Broadly speaking, normative instruments developed by international organisations need to be adopted or used domestically to have a legal and practical effect. The ways in which this is done depends on each countries' constitutional systems, and is often done without any involvement of IOs. Nevertheless, IOs may track the use of their instruments, and provide related support and guidance to their Members to implement them (OECD, 2019[1]).

The voluntary nature of international instruments entails that domestic regulatory authorities maintain a certain leeway in the interpretation and adaptation of the international text to the domestic context. The international nature of these standards entails that the implementation processes vary according to different legal systems.

Overall, a broad notion of "implementation" of voluntary international standards has two components: i) the de jure incorporation/ application of an international standard in domestic legislation, and ii) the de facto use made of the international standard in practice, either in the inspection and enforcement processes or by private companies in their production process (Combacau and Sur, 2016[10]). This same distinction is reflected by ISO's understanding of implementation:

"A normative document can be said to be "implemented" in two different ways. It may be applied in production, trade, etc., and it may be taken over, wholly or in part, in another normative document. Through the medium of this second document, it may then be applied, or it may again be taken over in yet another normative document."[3]

> The de facto use made of international standards entails the actual application of the standard by its end-users. Evidence of such use is usually harder to monitor by IO Secretariats, who are rarely in contact directly with citizens or economic actors.
>
> The de jure component of implementation is defined by ISO as the adoption or taking over of an international standard in a national normative document.[4] This implementation of international standards into domestic legislation depends on each country's domestic procedures. While supposedly easier to track (given the transparency requirements related to domestic laws and regulations), the de jure adoption of international standards in domestic legislation may take different forms (by reference to an international standard or a domestic standard reflecting international practice, by partial or complete text transcription…) and involve various degree of conformity with the international instrument that complicates its monitoring.
>
> [1] Oxford dictionary https://en.oxforddictionaries.com/definition/implementation.
> [2] www.lexisnexis.com/help/cu/CU.htm#The_Legislative_Process/Stage_9.htm.
> [3] ISO ISO/IEC Guide 2:2004 10.
> [4] ISO ISO/IEC Guide 2:2004, 10.1.
> Source: (OECD, 2019[11]), http://www.oecd.org/gov/regulatory-policy/IO-Rule-Based%20System.pdf; (Combacau and Sur, 2016[10]), Droit international public, LGDJ-Lextenso, https://www.lgdj.fr/droit-international-public-9782275045092.html (accessed 12 September 2018).

Implementation how?

The OIE Codes include a user's guide, guiding OIE Members in the use of the Codes. This user's guide specifies that the Codes should be used by competent authorities "to set up measures":

- User's Guide of the *Terrestrial Code*: "Veterinary Authorities should use the standards in the *Terrestrial Code* to set up measures providing for early detection, internal reporting, notification, control or eradication of pathogenic agents, including zoonotic ones, in terrestrial animals (mammals, birds, reptiles and bees) and preventing their spread via international trade in animals and animal products, while avoiding unjustified sanitary barriers to trade."[19]
- User's Guide of the *Aquatic Code*: "Competent Authorities should use the standards in the *Aquatic Code* to develop measures for early detection, internal reporting, notification, control or eradication of pathogenic agents in aquatic animals (amphibians, crustaceans, fish and molluscs) and preventing their spread via international trade in aquatic animals and aquatic animal products, while avoiding unjustified sanitary barriers to trade."[20]

In other words, the implementation of OIE standards require domestic legislation that should provide a basis for Competent Authorities to develop sanitary measures. Therefore, when implementing OIE standards, OIE Members give a legal effect at the domestic level to the conditions set at the international level by incorporating the standard in any domestic text, whether law, regulation or other normative act.

In addition, the OIE also provides various tools to assist Members in the development of sanitary measures, and the use of OIE standards in this context. These are mainly targeted guidelines on the implementation of specific standards.

In particular, the OIE has established guidelines for veterinary legislation,[21] which were subsequently adopted as standards in Chapter 3.4 of the *Terrestrial Code*, to assist Members in the implementation of OIE standards, for terrestrial animals, in the development of SPS measures. The relevant Code provisions establish general principles on the form, content and objectives of veterinary legislation. Among others, they recommend that OIE Members designate competent authorities to develop veterinary legislation following the OIE definition to do so, to hold an inventory of veterinary legislation and make it "… readily accessible and intelligible for use, updating and modification, as appropriate" (art. 3.4.3 *Terrestrial Code*). These recommendations apply to veterinary legislation in general and as such do not prescribe conformity with OIE standards, which remain voluntary. They do not explicitly provide any guidance on how to incorporate international standards into the veterinary legislation. However, several references are made to the OIE, including in the article 3.4.13 on technical recommendations on the legislation concerning import and export procedures and veterinary certification. This article recommend that veterinary legislation "should provide a basis for actions to address the elements relating to import and export procedures and veterinary certification referred to in Section 5."

Other guidance is provided for example in certain chapters of the terrestrial and aquatic Manuals, which set out procedures to be followed by laboratory workers in the control of vaccines or laboratory diagnosis of diseases. In addition, a specific set of guidelines is developed for the implementation of disease control programmes, in order to create an enabling regulatory and institutional environment for the eradication of a disease (OIE, 2014[5]). For examples of such guidance provisions, see Box 1.3.

Box 1.3. Examples of implementation guidance within OIE standards

A number of provisions developed by the OIE contain guidance on implementation of specific provisions of the OIE Codes or Manuals.

Introduction of the *Terrestrial Manual*:

> *"Each disease chapter includes a summary intended to provide information for veterinary officials and other readers who need a general overview of the tests and vaccines available for the disease. This is followed by a text giving greater detail for laboratory workers. In each disease chapter, Part A gives a general introduction to the disease, Part B deals with laboratory diagnosis of the disease, and Part C (where appropriate) with the requirements for vaccines or in vivo diagnostic biologicals. The information concerning production and control of vaccines or diagnostics is given as an example; it is not always necessary to follow these when there are scientifically justifiable reasons for using alternative approaches. Bibliographic references that provide further information are listed at the end of each chapter."*

Introduction to the *Aquatic Manual*:

> *"The general provisions and disease-specific recommendations of the Aquatic Manual together provide technical information to support implementation of standards contained in the OIE Aquatic Animal Health Code (Aquatic Code). These standards include Member countries' obligations to report the occurrence of listed diseases; requirements to demonstrate freedom for a country, zone or compartment; requirements for responding to the occurrence of a disease; and requirements to return to freedom following a disease outbreak. The recommendations in the Aquatic Manual and the Aquatic Code are intended to be complementary and both documents should be used together when developing or undertaking surveillance activities in accordance with OIE Standards."*

Source: (OIE, 2014[5]), *Guidelines for Animal Disease Control*,
http://www.oie.int/fileadmin/home/eng/our_scientific_expertise/docs/pdf/a_guidelines_for_animal_disease_control_final.pdf.

Beyond these guidance documents, however, the OIE does not promote a specific approach to the adoption of its standards in domestic legislation, leaving it to the specificity of each institutional framework. For example, it does not specify the form of legislation to be used (primary, secondary, or tertiary legislation). The choice of the form of legislation may have implications on the formality of the national measure, as primary legislation has a stronger legal stance, but implies debates in national parliaments and may thus result in a text quite different from the international standard. Secondary legislation is more technical, developed usually by the executive body or independent authorities, and may be easier to monitor. De facto, analytical work by the OIE on trade of aquatic animals and aquatic animal products shows that sanitary measures take different forms in countries (Figure 1.5). The OIE does not specify either the format of the reference to the OIE standard, leaving countries to choose for example between literal transposition of OIE standard, dated or non-dated reference to a specific standard, or copying of relevant language of the standard.

Figure 1.5. Classification of notified legislations according to their ranking in the hierarchy of legislation and their objective

Higher rank and power, but more difficult to change or modify

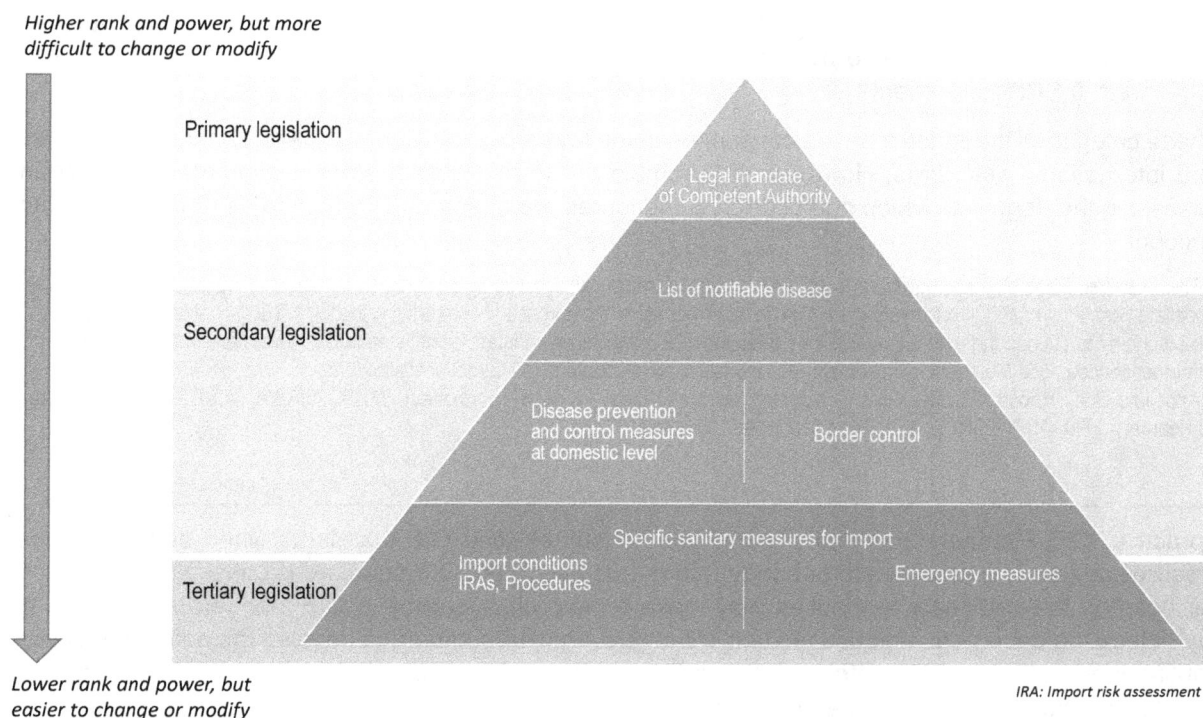

Lower rank and power, but easier to change or modify

IRA: Import risk assessment

Note: This schematic diagram was developed on the basis of the analysis of 148 legislations notified to WTO between 2007 and 2018.
Source: (Bucher, Tellechea and Mylrea, 2019[11]), "Safe trade of aquatic animals and aquatic animal products: exploring the use of OIE international standards for setting sanitary measures", *OIE Scientific and Technical Review*, Vol. 38/2.

The WTO SPS Agreement provides additional international commitments binding in the WTO legal order, requiring the use of OIE standards by WTO Members except where a higher level of protection is justified based on scientific justification/risk assessment.[22] In this context, the SPS Agreement envisages different levels of compliance of domestic regulations with international standards (see Box 1.4). However, beyond the text of the agreement, the WTO does not provide additional guidance to regulatory authorities on the practical approach to follow when considering international standards.

Box 1.4. Levels of implementation with international standards in WTO SPS Agreement

The WTO SPS Agreement envisages that for the purpose of complying with the WTO obligation of harmonisation, there are several levels of compliance with international standards:

- SPS measures "based on" international standard, i.e. reference to international standard in national legislation, regulations, etc. (art. 3.1 SPS Agreement). "Such a measure may adopt some, not necessarily all, of the elements of the international standard."[1]

- "Conformity" with international standard, i.e. identical transcription of international standard in text of national measure. "such a measure would embody the international standard completely and, for practical purposes, converts it into a municipal standard".[2] Measures which conform with international standards are "… deemed to be necessary to protect human, animal or plant life or health, and presumed to be consistent with the relevant provisions of this Agreement and of GATT 1994" (art. 3.2 SPS Agreement).

- Deviation from international standard: the WTO SPS Agreement also recognizes the possibility for WTO Members to adopt a level of protection higher than that embedded in an international standard, if it is justified by scientific evidence, or justified by a risk assessment (art. 3.3 and art. 5 SPS Agreement).

These categories introduce a notion of variation in the levels of consistency between national measures and international standards. However, they remain broad and do not provide concrete guidance on assessing the degree to which domestic SPS measures are based on OIE standards or take them into account.

1 The Appellate Body clarified that there is no "rule-exception" relationship between the three scenarios for the purposes of WTO law. Appellate Body Report, EC – Hormones, para. 104. In other words, for the purpose of complying with their WTO obligations, Members have the autonomy to choose the extent to which they base their SPS measures on international standards. Nevertheless, the wording of the agreement encourages Members to implement SPS measures which conform to international standards.

2 Appellate Body Report, EC Measures Concerning Meat and Meat Products (Hormones), WT/DS26/AB/R, WT/DS48/AB/R, adopted 13 February 1998, DSR 1998:I, p. 135. See Spec. para. 170 et seq.

In practice, OIE Members' veterinary authorities consult existing OIE standards when developing draft measures related to animal health or safety (Kahn, 2018[12]). If the OIE standard is considered relevant for their country, the veterinary authorities may make an explicit reference to OIE standards broadly in the preamble of the document, and use the text of the relevant OIE standard to develop the national measure, adapting it as necessary. The reference to the OIE standards does not always specify the exact standard that is used as a basis, in case the standard still evolves. In some cases, some countries chose to make a dated reference to an OIE standard, to clarify the version used for the particular text. Annex A provides insights into how countries typically embed OIE standards in their legislation, based on a questionnaire developed as part of a specific thematic item 1, for 86th General Session of the World Assembly of Delegates.

Implementation by whom?

In line with common IO practice, implementation of OIE standards is a shared responsibility between Members and the Secretariat (OECD, 2019[1]). The OIE Members are responsible for setting up the right measures within their domestic legal framework to reflect the OIE standards agreed on internationally, whereas the OIE Secretariat provides support and guidance to foster consistent understanding of OIE standards among its Members.

At the country level, the uptake of OIE standards into domestic legislation falls under the responsibility of the authorities tasked with the regulation of animal health and welfare. The OIE Glossary of the *Terrestrial Code* defines competent and veterinary authorities as follows:[23]

- "**Competent authority**": means the Veterinary Authority or other Governmental Authority of a Member Country having the responsibility and competence for ensuring or supervising the implementation of animal health and welfare measures, international veterinary certification and other standards and recommendations in the *Terrestrial Code* and in the OIE *Aquatic Animal Health Code* in the whole territory.

- "**Veterinary authority**": means the Governmental Authority of a Member Country, comprising veterinarians, other professionals and paraprofessionals, having the responsibility and competence for ensuring or supervising the implementation of animal health and welfare measures, international veterinary certification and other standards and recommendations in the *Terrestrial Code* in the whole territory.

The OIE 2018 questionnaire for technical item 1 of the 86th General Session indicates that the large majority of OIE Members have designated not one but several competent authorities in their country for developing sanitary measures to support market access (Figure 1.6). Nevertheless, in 93% of cases, a veterinary authority is involved, underlying consistency across countries' institutional frameworks likely to facilitate discussion and data collection between the secretariat and Members. In many cases, a variety of other authorities is still involved. This may require co-ordination efforts at the domestic level to ensure that OIE standards are evenly implemented by the different competent authorities.

The OIE Secretariat makes significant efforts to support its Members in implementing OIE standards, namely with the variety of tools described in Chapter 3. The OIE's World Assembly of Delegates, as the highest authority of the OIE bringing together all Member countries, is the main body in charge of overseeing from the highest political level the advocacy, assistance and monitoring of implementation of the standards. This is comparable to other IOs surveyed by the OECD in 2018, who in a majority of cases invest either a high-level body or a technical body of implementation-related tasks.[24]

Figure 1.6. Which is the designated competent authority in your country responsible for developing sanitary requirements applied to the importation of commodities?

145 respondents

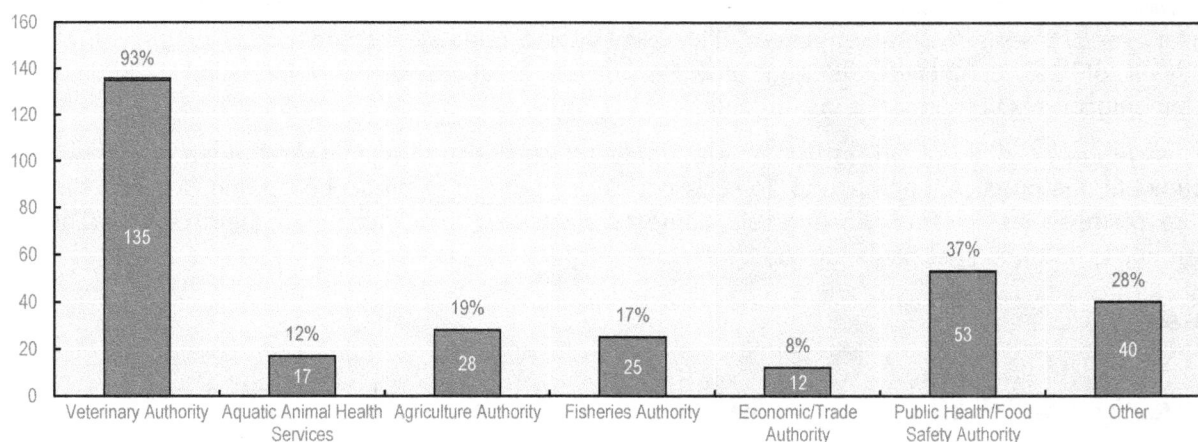

Note: The percentages do not add up to 100%, because respondents often included various competent authorities.
Source: OIE questionnaire Technical Item 1, 86th General Session, World Assembly, World Organisation for Animal Health, May 2018.

Conclusion: Key features of the body of OIE normative instruments

The OIE develops and maintains a corpus of different voluntary normative instruments. This corpus of instruments is largely dominated by Codes and Manuals, which follow the most comprehensive expert-driven procedure and are the most widely used by the Members among the OIE instruments. Logically, these Codes and Manuals are therefore also the normative instruments that are subject to monitoring of implementation. These monitoring mechanisms are the subject of Chapter 2.

Namely thanks to the expert-driven standard-setting procedure of the Codes and Manuals, these instruments remain highly technical, and serve as a support for OIE Members' veterinary authorities in the development of veterinary legislation as well as in the diagnosis of diseases. As such, they benefit from dynamic involvement of OIE Members through the various technical bodies that allow for expert discussions on new areas of scientific developments and in support of an active use of the OIE acquis.

Within the OIE corpus, the Official Recognition of Disease Status is a unique procedure established by the OIE for certain diseases that provides a normative statement by the organisation and reflects the outcome of implementation of the OIE *Terrestrial Code* and *Manual*. It can therefore be used as a reference by OIE Members to demonstrate compliance with OIE standards and gain access to export markets. More broadly, the maintenance of the status by a Member gives confidence and demonstrates the capabilities that the Member is able to comply with the OIE standards.

The OIE benefits from a largely monopolistic position within the international standards sphere of animal health, as no other international body sets standards in the precise same area, despite some common areas of work with other organisations such as the WHO and the Codex Alimentarius. The WTO SPS Agreement's recognition of the OIE's standards as a reference for animal health standards gives additional visibility to the OIE normative instruments and reinforces the incentives for countries to consider them more systematically when setting domestic veterinary legislation. Overall, the OIE's position as unique international standard-setting body in its field helps prevent duplication of international standards and simplifies domestic regulators' search for relevant international instruments in their drafting of veterinary legislation. In fine, these features should make easier OIE's task of tracking the use of their instruments in domestic regulatory measures.

In addition, the clear and well-defined mandate of the OIE combines with a rather homogenous set of bodies involved in the implementation of OIE standards at the domestic level. Indeed, a large majority of OIE Members have veterinary authorities involved in the development of national measures setting sanitary requirements for market access. This allows for a relatively homogeneous landscape across countries of OIE contact points and provides for an ideal source of information regarding the implementation of OIE normative instruments.

Still, while the adoption of OIE instruments in domestic legislation is encouraged by various normative documents, the practical approach to do so is not clearly defined or prescribed owing to their voluntary nature of these instruments. As a result, domestic measures may implement them only partially or differently to adapt to specific conditions.

Notes

[1] For further details on the objectives of the OIE, see www.oie.int/about-us/our-missions/.

[2] https://www.oie.int/fileadmin/home/eng/media_center/docs/pdf/fact_sheets/en_normes.pdf.

[3] *Terrestrial Animal Health Code* available at www.oie.int/en/standard-setting/terrestrial-code/access-online/.

Aquatic Animal Health Code available at www.oie.int/en/standard-setting/aquatic-code/access-online/.

[4] *Terrestrial Manual* available at www.oie.int/en/standard-setting/terrestrial-manual/access-online/.

Aquatic Manual available at www.oie.int/en/standard-setting/aquatic-manual/access-online/.

[5] General Rules of the World Organisation for Animal Health (Articles 1, 50, 59, 60).

[6] See Introduction (How to Use This Terrestrial Manual) at www.oie.int/standard-setting/terrestrial-manual/access-online/; and foreword for Aquatic Manual, at www.oie.int/index.php?id=2439&L=0&htmfile=avant-propos.htm.

[7] Terms of reference and internal rules of the regional commissions and regional conferences. See www.oie.int/fileadmin/home/eng/about_us/docs/pdf/basic_text/80%20sg19_basictexts_ang%20part%202.pdf.

[8] The list of MoUs concluded by the OIE are here: www.oie.int/en/about-us/key-texts/cooperation-agreements/.

[9] www.oie.int/about-us/wo/council/.

[10] The terrestrial animal health standards commission; the scientific commission for animal diseases; the biological standards commission; and the aquatic animal health standards commission. www.oie.int/about-us/wo/commissions-master/.

www.oie.int/standard-setting/specialists-commissions-working-ad-hoc-groups/working-groups-reports/.

[12] www.oie.int/scientific-expertise/collaborating-centres/terms-of-reference/.

[13] www.oie.int/scientific-expertise/reference-laboratories/terms-of-reference/.

[14] www.oie.int/about-us/wo/headquarters/.

[15] www.oie.int/en/about-us/director-general-office/strategic-plan/.

[16] These work programmes are included in the meeting reports of each Specialist commission, available at www.oie.int/standard-setting/specialists-commissions-working-ad-hoc-groups/scientific-commission-reports/meetings-reports/.

[17]
www.oie.int/fileadmin/home/eng/about_us/docs/pdf/basic_text/80%20sg19_basictexts_ang%20part%202.pdf.

[18] Art 5 of Appendix to International Agreement of the OIE, www.oie.int/about-us/key-texts/basic-texts/international-agreement-for-the-creation-of-an-office-international-des-epizooties/.

[19] www.oie.int/index.php?id=169&L=0&htmfile=guide.htm.

[20] www.oie.int/index.php?id=171&L=0&htmfile=guide.htm.

[21] www.oie.int/fileadmin/home/eng/support_to_oie_members/docs/pdf/a_guidelines_vetleg.pdf.

[22] See articles 3 and 5 of the SPS Agreement.

[23] www.oie.int/fileadmin/home/eng/health_standards/aahc/2010/en_glossaire.htm#terme_autorite_veterinaire. See a similar definition under the Glossary of the Aquatic Code at www.oie.int/index.php?id=171&L=0&htmfile=glossaire.htm.

[24] OECD 2018 IO Survey.

References

Bucher, K., D. Tellechea and G. Mylrea (2019), "Safe trade of aquatic animals and aquatic animal products: exploring the use of OIE international standards for setting sanitary measures", *OIE Scientific and Technical Review*, Vol. 38/2.   [11]

Combacau, J. and S. Sur (2016), *Droit international public*, LGDJ-Lextenso, https://www.lgdj.fr/droit-international-public-9782275045092.html (accessed on 12 September 2018).   [10]

Kahn, B. (2018), *Implementation of OIE Standards by OIE Member Countries: State of Play and Specific Capacity Building Needs. Descriptive Analysis of the Questionnaire*.   [12]

OECD (2019), *The Contribution of International Organisations to a Rule-Based International System*, OECD, Paris, http://www.oecd.org/gov/regulatory-policy/IO-Rule-Based%20System.pdf.   [1]

OECD (2016), *International Regulatory Co-operation: The Role of International Organisations in Fostering Better Rules of Globalisation*, OECD Publishing, Paris, https://dx.doi.org/10.1787/9789264244047-en.   [2]

OECD/WTO (2019), *Facilitating Trade through Regulatory Cooperation: The Case of the WTO's TBT/SPS Agreements and Committees*, OECD Publishing, Paris/World Trade Organization, Geneva, https://dx.doi.org/10.1787/ad3c655f-en.   [3]

OIE (2019), *OIE Tool for the Evaluation of Performance of Veterinary Services, PVS Tool, Seventh Edition*, http://www.oie.int/fileadmin/Home/eng/Support_to_OIE_Members/pdf/AF-PVSTool.pdf.   [8]

OIE (2018), *Guidelines for Investigation of Suspicious Biological Events (Guidelines for National Veterinary Services)*, http://www.oie.int/fileadmin/Home/eng/Our_scientific_expertise/docs/pdf/Guidelines_Investigation_Suspicious_Biological_Events.pdf.   [6]

OIE (2018), *OIE List of Antimicrobial Agents of Veterinary Importance*, http://www.oie.int/fileadmin/Home/eng/Our_scientific_expertise/docs/pdf/AMR/A_OIE_List_antimicrobials_May2018.pdf.   [9]

OIE (2016), *Procedures used by the OIE to set standards and recommendations for international trade, with a focus on the Terrestrial and aquatic animal health codes*, http://www.oie.int/fileadmin/Home/eng/Internationa_Standard_Setting/docs/pdf/A_OIE_procedures_standards_2016.pdf.   [4]

OIE (2014), *Guidelines for Animal Disease Control*, http://www.oie.int/fileadmin/home/eng/our_scientific_expertise/docs/pdf/a_guidelines_for_animal_disease_control_final.pdf.   [5]

OIE (2013), *Veterinary Education Core Curriculum, OIE Guidelines*, http://www.oie.int/Veterinary_Education_Core_Curriculum.pdf.   [7]

2 Existing mechanisms supporting and monitoring the implementation of OIE standards

This chapter takes stock of the mechanisms that currently exist within the OIE or beyond that are used, or may be used, to gather information on the implementation of OIE standards in domestic jurisdictions. The current chapter finds 13 such mechanisms, most of which are set up by the OIE itself, and others that exist in the context of the World Trade Organisation or of the European Union for example. These mechanisms were initially set up to address specific needs, such as evaluating the quality and building domestic capacity of veterinary services, or monitoring the effects of domestic regulations on trade among others. Therefore the information they provide on the implementation of OIE standards is limited in scope and irregular in frequency. This chapter identifies the extent to which these existing mechanisms can be used to feed into the work of the OIE observatory and where further information is needed.

Various internal and external mechanisms already exist that look into country implementation practices of OIE standards, namely with three major objectives: to monitor countries' animal health and welfare systems, to monitor OIE Member countries' sanitary status, and to monitor the impact of veterinary measures on trade. In addition, a number of mechanisms monitor implementation on specific regional or thematic issues. While OIE monitoring mechanisms mainly pursue the first two objectives, impacts on international trade are mainly monitored through WTO mechanisms. The EU Commission has one mechanism monitoring among others the animal health legislation within EU Member countries.

Figure 2.1 synthetises mechanisms that collect information of relevance to OIE normative instruments. Most monitor areas related to the OIE Codes. Much less are related to the implementation of OIE Manuals. Overall, and from a very preliminary mapping, the existing OIE mechanisms cover around a quarter of the OIE Codes and Manuals.[1] The Thematic items of the World Assembly of Delegates (WAD) do not have a pre-defined scope of standards they apply to and may cover all and any of the OIE acquis. The mechanisms of the WTO and the EU Commission do not specify the OIE normative instruments, but relate to the OIE Codes and Manuals in a broad sense.

Figure 2.1. Overview of potential "monitoring" mechanisms and their relevance to OIE standards

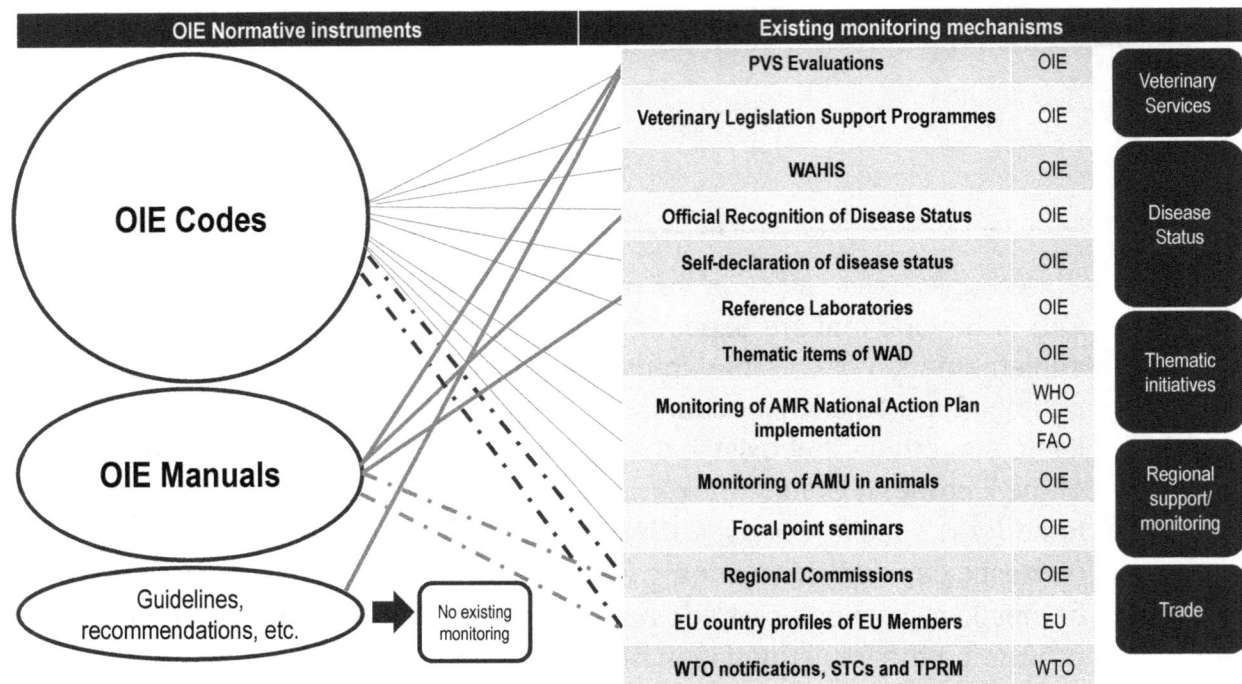

Notes: The full lines show monitoring of instruments as it is officially provided for in texts or terms of reference. The dotted lines provide indication of possible monitoring, despite no explicit mention of the normative instruments.
Source: Author's own elaboration.

Overall, a wealth of information is gathered through these mechanisms, used extensively by countries to improve their own veterinary systems, evaluate the veterinary situation of their trading partners and to reinforce trust of trading partners in their own veterinary systems. These are not mechanisms monitoring or evaluating implementation per se (see Box 2.1). Indeed, the information is generally not collected with a view to assess the uptake of OIE standards in national legislation, but rather as a result of mechanisms set in different backgrounds, with different objectives, and conducted by different authorities (whether in the OIE or outside). Consequently, these mechanisms function mostly in silos, without much overlaps or coordination, and without an explicit role of feeding in to the standard-setting process. Nevertheless, they provide an invaluable resource for the OIE Observatory insofar as they gather significant information on implementation of OIE standards. They may still require readjustments to ensure that the information is adequate to serve the purpose of the Observatory.

Box 2.1. Defining monitoring and evaluation

Notwithstanding their complementarity, monitoring and evaluation are two different practices, with different dynamics and goals (OECD, 2019[1]). There is no internationally agreed definition of either term, but practice from the national policymaking context can be used to understand the concepts of monitoring and evaluation of international rules and standards.

Monitoring is used to designate a systematic collection, analysis and presentation of information/ data to gather indications of the extent of progress and achievement of objectives in relation to an agreed schedule.[1] Policy monitoring in particular refers to a continuous function that uses systematic data collection on specific indicators to provide policy makers and stakeholders with information regarding progress and achievements of an ongoing public policy initiative and/or the use of allocated funds (OECD, 2016[2]). Policy monitoring therefore contributes to planning and operational decision making, as it provides evidence to measure performance and can help to raise specific questions in order to identify implementation delays or bottlenecks. It can also strengthen accountability related to the use of resources, the efficiency of internal management processes, or the outputs of a given policy initiative (OECD, 2017[3]).

Evaluation of domestic laws and regulations can be done either ex ante, to identify likely costs and benefits of a regulatory or non regulatory option for a policy under consideration, or ex post, assessing the effectiveness of policies or regulations once they are in force (OECD, 2018[4]). The evaluation of the implementation of international standards can be assimilated to *ex post* evaluation of laws and regulations at the national level. Such evaluation consists in examining the relevance, effectiveness, and impacts of regulatory decisions, as well as, identifying unintended outcomes, reason for failure, and factors contributing to success (OECD, 2016[5]). Policy evaluation at the national level is found to serve two main purposes. It fosters learning by helping policy makers understand why and how a policy was successful or not. Consequently, it contributes to strategic decision-making, by providing insights on how to improve the links between policy decisions and outcomes. In addition, policy evaluation promotes accountability as it provides citizens and a broad range of stakeholders – such as journalists and academics - with information whether the efforts carried out by the government, including the financial resources mobilised for them, are producing the expected results (OECD, 2017[3]).

1 See definitions of monitoring for specific contexts in (OECD, 2010[6]), (OECD, 2018[4]) and (Eurostat, 2014[7]).
Source: (OECD, 2019[1]); (OECD, 2016[2]); (OECD, 2017[3]); (OECD, 2018[4]); (OECD, 2016[5]); (OECD, 2017[3]).

Mechanisms collecting information on countries' animal health and welfare system: the PVS Pathway

Quality of veterinary services lay the institutional foundation for an effective implementation of OIE standards at the national level. The Veterinary Services are "the governmental and non-governmental organisations that implement animal health and welfare measures and other standards and recommendations in the *Terrestrial Code* and the OIE *Aquatic Animal Health Code* in the territory (…)."[2] The OIE therefore set up a complex system for evaluating the quality of veterinary services, by specific experts trained and certified by the OIE.

The OIE PVS Pathway is a general programme that aims to ensure that OIE Members' veterinary services are capable of implementing OIE standards. It entails several steps to make an assessment of country's veterinary systems (through a PVS Evaluation), make recommendations to improve them (through a PVS Gap Analysis) and to assist in the reinforcement of the veterinary services (through veterinary legislation support programmes, or other targeted capacity building activities).

Figure 2.2. OIE PVS Pathway

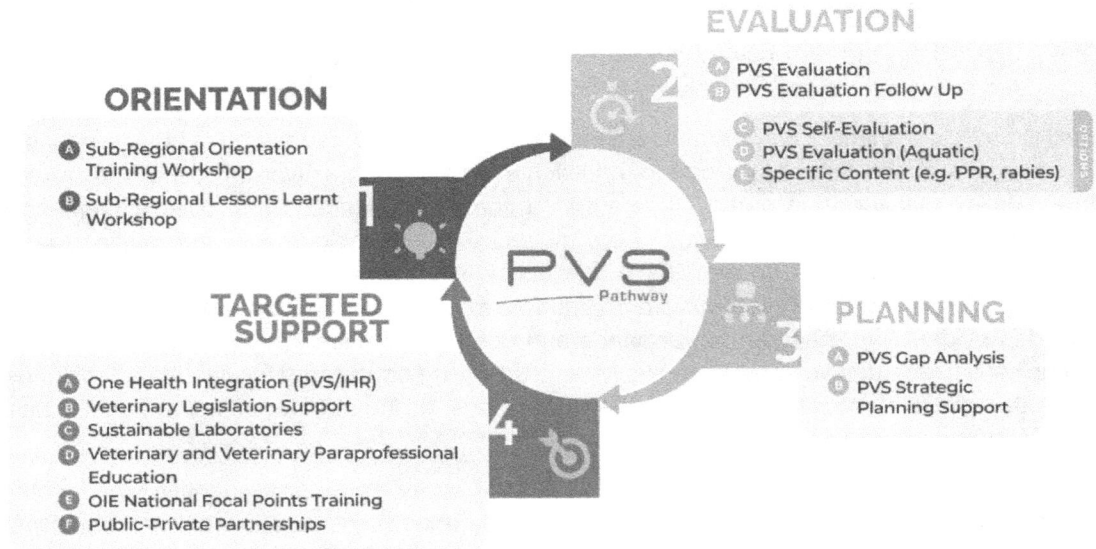

Source: (OIE, 2019[8]), "OIE Tool for the Evaluation of Performance of Veterinary Services", 7th edition, http://www.oie.int/fileadmin/home/eng/support_to_oie_members/pdf/af-pvstool.pdf.

The normative framework, i.e. the OIE standards setting criteria for quality veterinary services, are found in the OIE *Terrestrial* and *Aquatic Code*s, and serve as a basis in the conduct of the valuations:

- *Terrestrial Code*: Section 3[3] is specifically dedicated to the quality of veterinary services. This Section covers fundamental principles applicable to veterinary services (Chapter 3.1), the principles and criteria for the evaluation of veterinary services (Chapter 3.2), communication by veterinary services (Chapter 3.3) and the procedure and institutional setting necessary for the development of veterinary legislation (Chapter 3.4). In addition, a number of articles throughout the Code include specific standards applicable to veterinary services.

- *Aquatic Code*: Section 3[4] is briefer than the *Terrestrial Code*, and is specifically dedicated to the quality of aquatic animal health services (Chapter 3.1) and communication by veterinary services (Chapter 3.2).

PVS Evaluations systematically assess the quality of Veterinary Services, including their implementation of the OIE standards by Veterinary Services. In addition, specific procedures exist to assess use of OIE standards in veterinary legislation, through the Veterinary legislation support programme. The subsequent stages in the PVS Pathway help address the challenges identified in the Evaluations, allowing OIE Members to improve their implementation of the standards. The PVS Evaluation Follow-up missions then serve as a stocktaking of the progress made since the initial evaluation.

PVS Evaluations

PVS Evaluations are conducted on a voluntary basis at the request of OIE Member Countries. They involve an OIE certified team of 2-4 experts undertaking a 1-4 week mission (depending on size and complexity of the country) and assessing all aspects of Veterinary Services capacity via documentation review, field interviews and observations. A peer-reviewed PVS report is presented for country comments and finalisation.

Table 2.1. State of play of PVS Evaluation missions

As of 4 September 2018

OIE Region	Requests received (number of countries)[1]	Missions implemented	Reports available for restricted distribution to Donors and Partners	Reports available on the OIE website
Africa	53	51	33	11
Americas	27	26	10	9
Asia/ Pacific	28	27	11	4
Europe	20	20	10	2
Middle East	13	11	5	1
Total	**141**	**135**	**69**	**27**

[1] The Members having requested PVS Evaluation missions are the following:

Africa (53): Algeria, Angola, Benin, Botswana, Burkina Faso, Burundi, Cameroon, Cape Verde, Central African Rep., Chad, Comoros, Rep. of the Congo, Dem. Rep. of the Congo, Côte d'Ivoire, Djibouti, Egypt, Equatorial Guinea, Eritrea, Ethiopia, Gabon, Gambia, Ghana, Guinea, Guinea-Bissau, Kenya, Lesotho, Liberia, Libya, Madagascar, Malawi, Mali, Mauritania, Mauritius, Morocco, Mozambique, Namibia, Niger, Nigeria, Rwanda, São Tomé and Principe, Senegal, Seychelles, Sierra Leone, Somalia, South Africa, Sudan, Swaziland, Tanzania, Togo, Tunisia, Uganda, Zambia, Zimbabwe.
Americas (27): Argentina, Bahamas, Barbados, Belize, Bolivia, Brazil, Canada, Chile, Colombia, Costa Rica, Dominican Rep., Ecuador, El Salvador, Guatemala, Guyana, Haiti, Honduras, Jamaica, Mexico, Nicaragua, Panama, Paraguay, Peru, Suriname, Trinidad and Tobago, Uruguay, Venezuela.
Asia-Pacific (28): Australia, Bangladesh, Bhutan, Brunei, Cambodia, Chinese Taipei, Fiji, India, Indonesia, Iran, Japan, Dem. People's Rep. of Korea, Laos, Maldives, Malaysia, Mongolia, Myanmar, Nepal, New Caledonia, Pakistan, Papua New Guinea, Philippines, Sri Lanka, Thailand, Timor Leste, Vanuatu, Vietnam.
Europe (20): Albania, Armenia, Azerbaijan, Belarus, Bosnia and Herzegovina, Bulgaria, Former Yugolsav Republic of Macedonia, Georgia, Iceland, Israel, Kazakhstan, Kyrgyzstan, Montenegro, Romania, Serbia, Tajikistan, Turkey, Turkmenistan, Ukraine, Uzbekistan.
Middle-East (13): Afghanistan, Bahrein, Iraq, Jordan, Kuwait, Lebanon, Oman, Palestinian National Authority (observer), Qatar, Saudi Arabia, Syria, United Arab Emirates, Yemen.
Source: http://www.oie.int/solidarity/pvs-evaluations/status-of-missions/.

So far they have mostly occurred in developing countries.[5] However, developed countries are increasingly requesting PVS Evaluations. Recent cases have included Australia, Japan and Canada. Iceland and Mexico.[6] To date, 135 evaluation missions have been conducted, 50 of which have been the subject of PVS Evaluation follow-up missions.

PVS Evaluations involve some costs for the evaluated Members, who cover the venues and transport of the mission teams in their country and need dedicated staff to co-ordinate the PVS Evaluation. PVS Pathway expert costs are generally covered by the OIE, via their donor funded Animal Health and Welfare Fund, except for developed or other countries ineligible for donor support. Some regions benefit more frequently from PVS missions than others, depending on Member country and donor interest.

PVS Evaluations are conducted following the *OIE Tool for the Evaluation of Performance of Veterinary Services* (the "*OIE PVS Tool*) updated in 2019 (OIE, 2019[8]), and the *OIE PVS Tool: Aquatic*. These two tools describe the methodology for conducting evaluations of Veterinary Services in line with the standards included in the OIE *Terrestrial* and *Aquatic Code*s (cf. spec. Chapter 3.2 *Terrestrial Code on evaluation*). An update of the PVS Tool has been finalised in 2018, and published in 2019 as the seventh edition of the PVS Tool. A process to update Chapters 3.1 and 3.2 of the *Terrestrial Code* has also been initiated.

The evaluations are conducted against four Fundamental Components, broken down into "Critical Competencies", defined in-depth in the PVS Tool, with references to the specific OIE standards applicable. For each Critical Competency, a list of indicators is used by the assessors to determine countries' qualitative "level of advancement", i.e. the level of compliance with the OIE standards. In general, the levels of advancement range from 1 (no or limited capacity/capability) to 5 (high capacity and capability, fully compliant with international standards). The criteria for evaluating the level of advancement for each critical competency is defined in the PVS Tool. Each PVS Evaluation report includes a table summarising the evaluation results for all critical competencies.[7]

PVS Evaluation follow-up missions use the same methodology as the initial PVS Evaluation missions. They use as a baseline the level of advancement at the time of the initial PVS Evaluation mission, and the expected level of advancement identified in the PVS Gap Analysis. Like in the PVS Evaluation, an overall Summary of OIE PVS evaluation results is available.[8]

Six critical competencies in particular provide an overview of the status of implementation of OIE standards specific to veterinary legislation and regulations and access to markets. The principles of each of these six critical competencies are described in Box 2.2.

Box 2.2. Critical competencies related to veterinary legislation and market access

IV-1 Veterinary legislation

A. Legal quality and coverage

The authority and capability of the VS to develop or update veterinary legislation to ensure its quality and coverage of the veterinary domain.

This competency covers the quality of legislation considering the principles of legal drafting, its impact, and suitability for implementation.

This competency includes formal collaboration with other legal drafting professionals, other relevant ministries and Competent Authorities, national agencies and decentralised institutions that share authority or have mutual interest in relevant areas of the veterinary domain. It also covers stakeholder consultation relevant to veterinary legislation.

B. Implementation and compliance

The authority and capability of the VS to ensure compliance with legislation and regulations across the veterinary domain through communications and compliance inspection activities.

This competency includes formal collaboration with other relevant ministries and Competent Authorities, national agencies and decentralised institutions that share responsibility for implementation, or have mutual interest in relevant areas.

IV-3 International harmonisation

The authority and capability of the VS to be active in the harmonisation of national regulations and sanitary measures to ensure they take into account international standards, and/or related regional directives or guidelines.

IV-4 International certification

The authority and capability of the VS to reliably certify animals and animal products, and related services and processes under their mandate, for export, in accordance with national legislation and regulations, international standards and importing country requirements.

This refers to the country's veterinary export certification processes. Issues such as: the legislative basis, format and content of veterinary certificates; who signs certificates and the confidence they have in what they are certifying; and the outcome in terms of meeting international standards and/or importing country requirements to facilitate exportation should all be considered.

IV-5 Equivalence and other types of sanitary requirements

The authority and capability of the VS to apply flexibility in negotiating, implementing and maintaining equivalence and other types of sanitary agreements with trading partners.

IV-6 Transparency

The authority and capability of the VS to notify the OIE, WTO, trading partners and other relevant organisations of its disease status, regulations and sanitary measures and systems, in accordance with established procedures, as applicable to international trade.

Source: (OIE, 2013[9]), "OIE Tool for the Evaluation of Performance of Veterinary Services", 6th Edition, www.oie.int/fileadmin/Home/eng/Support_to_OIE_Members/pdf/PVS_A_Tool_Final_Edition_2013.pdf.

Overall, the PVS Evaluations are an important source of country-level information, focused on the systems or "horizontal" chapters of the OIE Codes. The PVS Evaluations provide an in-depth understanding of existing veterinary system in OIE Members. They provide less information at the detailed disease level of the "vertical" chapters. The PVS methodology details levels of advancement of assessed Members, providing an indication of the consistency between national legislation and OIE standards. When complemented by follow-up missions, the evaluations provide information on the evolution of implementation of the standards over time. However, this information is incomplete for the purposes of the OIE observatory, in terms of geographic scope, time coverage, and assessment of the use of the standards.

The geographic scope of the evaluations is limited to the countries requesting a PVS Evaluation. In particular, PVS Evaluations do not cover any of the EU countries for which EU regulatory processes exist. As a result, there is no overall assessment of all OIE Member Countries, making it difficult to draw broad assessments on trends of implementation by OIE Members as a whole. The evaluation is not systematic nor regular, as it depends on countries' requests. The information about implementation of OIE standards is therefore limited to a single period in time, which may be updated with information in a follow-up mission. Although the evaluations take as a baseline OIE standards, to assess situations in individual countries, the evaluation mostly relies on field missions, interviews and general research about the country, rather than assessment of disease-specific national measures in comparison with OIE standards.

In addition, the use of this information for monitoring purpose raises a number of challenges. The OIE Secretariat does not keep a centralised source of information to identify trends among OIE Members. The reports are kept in PDF formats, which make comparisons difficult to conduct. In order to address this issue, the OIE is currently designing a database of PVS evaluation reports that will facilitate the search of evidence and data from these reports.

The PVS Evaluation and follow-up mission reports are only made available to the public upon authorisation of the evaluated country. Evaluated countries may choose to make the report available to the general public on the OIE website, to keep distribution limited to donors and partners, or to restrict the publicity of the reports completely. In practice, availability to the public is still quite ad hoc (30 out of 135 PVS

Evaluation reports are available on the OIE website). In more than half the cases, the evaluated country choses to make the report available only to donors and partners (69 reports out of 135 PVS missions). There is an on-going initiative to facilitate accessibility to existing PVS Pathway mission reports. However, the secretariat, including after consultation with its Members, feels that the possibility of keeping the PVS reports confidential is an important component of the trust established between the organisation and its Members. This does not prevent the use of information for analytical purposes and in aggregate form.

Veterinary Legislation Support Programme (VLSP)

The VLSP is a component of the PVS Pathway. It consists of two components, the veterinary legislation identification missions (VLIM) and the veterinary legislation Agreement. The VLIMs are an opportunity to train regulators to more systematically consider international standards, and in particular OIE standards, in their regulatory process. In this process, the OIE Secretariat can gain more in-depth understanding on the veterinary legislation in OIE Members, and can thus gather additional evidence on the use of OIE standards to complement the information gathered during PVS Evaluation missions.

VLIM are launched at the request of OIE Members, as a follow-up to PVS Evaluations. This means that countries having undergone a VLIM are a subset of countries that have benefited from an initial PVS Evaluation mission. A total of 62 VLIM missions have been conducted to date, only in developing countries.[9] For only six of these are the reports publically available (Burundi, Chad, Ghana, Kenya, Mozambique, Rwanda).

The VLIM is an opportunity to undertake a detailed assessment of veterinary legislation in the country. In these missions, certified OIE VLSP experts assess the country's veterinary legislation against the standards for veterinary legislation as listed in Chapter 3.4 of the *Terrestrial Code*. This includes general principles (such as the respect for the hierarchy of legislation, legal basis, transparency, consultation, and the quality of legislation and legal certainty), as well as specific provisions on the drafting of the articles.

The methodology to follow for the VLSP is explained in three Manuals for experts:

- The first manual lays down general considerations on legal drafting, as provided in Chapter 3.4 of the *Terrestrial Code*. The manual goes point by point on the issues to be considered when assessing a country's legislation in order to ensure compliance with the relevant standards of the *Terrestrial Code*.
- The second manual sets the procedure of the mission: the team identifies in advance of the mission who they might need to speak to and other necessary information, for instance by consulting the database Faolex[10] for existing legislation in the country. The experts send out questionnaires on the legislative domain, with specific questions on the existence of legislation in the different areas of the Codes.
- The third manual provides working examples of veterinary legislation, to illustrate the key elements that may be included in a law, with a preamble, definitions, etc.

The VLIM missions are usually a week long, and composed of two experts, a veterinarian and a lawyer, who submit their report within a month after the mission. The report is sent back to the country delegates who can comment and ask for changes. If there is willingness and sufficient infrastructure to further improve the veterinary legislation, the OIE may conclude with the Member country a Veterinary Legislation Agreement, in which the OIE supports the country in amending existing legislation or drafting new legislation to address the recommendations set in the identification mission.[11]

In the same line as the PVS Evaluations, however, the evidence gathered during Veterinary Legislation Identification mission remains for the specific use of the evaluated OIE Member, suffering similar limitations. The scope of information remains limited to mostly developing countries, and the evaluations are not regular, therefore failing to provide a continuous state of play. Questionnaires examine compliance with certain horizontal chapters of the Codes (those listed in Chapter 3.4), asking countries to provide information on the relevant legislation in force. The use of disease-specific OIE standards is not assessed in specific national legislation. Like for PVS Evaluations, the final report is made public only if the evaluated country allows it. In some cases, the evaluated country choses to make their report available only to donors and partners.

Mechanisms to collect information on the sanitary status of OIE listed diseases for country, zone or compartment

One of the key objectives of the OIE is to ensure continuous transparency of disease outbreaks and all kinds of epidemiological events in their Member countries. To do so, the OIE has set up several tools through which OIE Members can be informed of the disease status in other countries.

The World Animal Health Information System (WAHIS) and the Self-Declarations provide mechanisms for reporting the status of diseases in OIE Members, based on countries self assessment and declaration. For six diseases, the OIE acts as an independent third party, and offers an official disease status recognition to OIE Members. This information is extensively used to facilitate trade between OIE Members. WAHIS and the OIE official disease status entail regular updates. The self-declarations are published by date, and are listed as "active", "temporary" or "not active.

In addition, to support countries in diagnosing diseases and gathering information at the local level, the OIE has set up Reference Laboratories, with designated experts that serve as a reference to all authorities within a country or region needing support in the diagnosis and control of diseases. While they do not have a mandate to monitor implementation of OIE standards per se, they gather relevant information when conducting testing or diagnoses for diseases; they have an obligation to inform the OIE WAHIS team of disease outbreaks; and their annual reports cover trends in implementation of OIE standards.

World Animal Health Information System (WAHIS)

The necessary information is gathered through mandatory notifications by OIE Members of first occurrence, recurrence or a sudden change related to a listed disease, infection or infestation, as well as an emerging disease, in a country, a zone or a compartment, as requested by articles 1.1.3-1.1.4 of both the *Terrestrial* and *Aquatic Code*s (Box 2.3). The notifications entail information about the first occurrence, recurrence or sudden changes related to OIE-listed diseases, as defined in disease-specific chapters of both Codes, as well as about the type of disease preventive and control measures. The national legislations themselves are not shared through the WAHIS notifications; it is a procedure of reporting via codified templates.

In other words, the WAHIS notifications allow to gather information on the implementation of articles 1.1.3-1.1.4 (notification obligation), on the diseases as defined by the Codes (Volume II of the *Terrestrial Code*; Sections 8, 9, 10, 11 of *Aquatic Code*) and on preventive and control measures.

Notifications by OIE Members are submitted in different timeframes depending on the type of measures:

- Notifications in real time (under 24 hours): occurrence, recurrence or sudden change in listed diseases;
- Weekly reports: "to provide further information on the evolution of the event which justified the notification. These reports should continue until the disease, infection or infestation has been eradicated or the situation has become sufficiently stable";
- Notifications every six months: "on the absence or presence and evolution of listed diseases".

In addition, the World Animal Health Information and Analysis Department (WAHIAD) also actively tracks "rumours" regarding disease outbreaks. If outbreaks occur and have not been notified to WAHIS, the Secretariat contacts the delegate of the country concerned to encourage notification. The Secretariat does not, however, have the authority to invalidate a notification or submit information to the public itself. The notified information is available to the general public on the WAHIS interface webpage.[12] Interested parties may choose to get WAHIS alerts directly on mobile phone devices.[13]

Box 2.3. WAHIS notification provisions, *Terrestrial Code*

Article 1.1.3.

Veterinary Authorities shall, under the responsibility of the Delegate, send to the Headquarters:

1. In accordance with relevant provisions in the disease-specific chapters, notification, through the World Animal Health Information System (WAHIS) or by fax or email within 24 hours, of any of the following events:

   a) first occurrence of a listed disease, infection or infestation in a country, a zone or a compartment;

   b) recurrence of a listed disease, infection or infestation in a country, a zone or a compartment following the final report that declared the outbreak ended;

   c) first occurrence of a new strain of a pathogenic agent of a listed disease, infection or infestation in a country, a zone or a compartment;

   d) a sudden and unexpected change in the distribution or increase in incidence or virulence of, or morbidity or mortality caused by, the pathogenic agent of a listed disease, infection or infestation present within a country, a zone or a compartment;

   e) occurrence of a listed disease, infection or infestation in an unusual host species.

2. Weekly reports subsequent to a notification under point 1) above, to provide further information on the evolution of the event which justified the notification. These reports should continue until the disease, infection or infestation has been eradicated or the situation has become sufficiently stable so that six-monthly reporting under point 3) will satisfy the obligation of the Member country; for each event notified, a final report should be submitted;

3. Six-monthly reports on the absence or presence and evolution of listed diseases, infections or infestations and information of epidemiological significance to other Member countries;

4. Annual reports concerning any other information of significance to other Member countries.

Article 1.1.4.

Veterinary Authorities shall, under the responsibility of the Delegate, send to the Headquarters:

5. A notification through WAHIS or by fax or email, when an emerging disease has been detected in a country, a zone or a compartment;

6. Periodic reports subsequent to a notification of an emerging disease:

   a) for the time necessary to have reasonable certainty that:

      i. the disease, infection or infestation has been eradicated; or

      ii. the situation has become stable;

OR

   b) until sufficient scientific information is available to determine whether it meets the criteria for inclusion in the OIE list as described in Chapter 1.2

   c) A final report once point 2 a) or b) above is complied with.

Source: OIE Terrestrial Code, www.oie.int/index.php?id=169&L=0&htmfile=chapitre_notification.htm.

The WAHIS notification system is unique in providing continuous information on factual situations regarding OIE listed diseases throughout OIE Member countries, outbreaks and changes to disease situations. Thanks to its relation to specific diseases listed in OIE Codes and related control measures, the WAHIS procedure has great potential to support the monitoring of implementation of notification obligations.

Nevertheless, the notification process would need to be adapted to allow for tracking implementation of OIE standards. In particular, the WAHIS notification procedures make few direct references to the *Terrestrial* or *Aquatic Code*s for each of the disease prevention and control measures.[14] This prevents from clearly monitoring the implementation of specific standards, and from making an automatic referencing of implementation. In addition, there is no detail on the control and prevention measures. The notification procedure only asks to tick boxes on the types of measures adopted and does not allow to identify the national legislation in which OIE standards are being implemented.

Self-declaration of disease status

Beyond the regular reporting through the WAHIS database, countries may choose to make a more in-depth self-declaration of their disease status for both aquatic and terrestrial diseases, according to art. 1.6 of the *Terrestrial Code* and 1.4. of the *Aquatic Code*. Contrary to official recognition of disease statuses, described below, these self-declarations are reviewed but not scrutinised in the same depths by the OIE Secretariat or Members before being published. They may be submitted by any OIE Member. By early 2019, there were 176 self-declarations available on the OIE website from 60 countries (30 OECD countries and 30 non-OECD ones).[15]

The self-declarations must include a list of information, including evidence on compliance with the disease-specific standards of the *Terrestrial* and *Aquatic Code*s (OIE, 2019, p. 5 et seq[10]). The standard operating procedures for self-declarations are not included in the Codes and can therefore be modified more flexibly.

The Disease Status Department (DSD) reviews the self-declaration and may choose to request further information, clarification, or update from WAHID, and may edit it as relevant. After the DSD and the delegate agree on the text, the Deputy Director General reviews the self-declaration, and decides if the self-declaration is acceptable for publication. If not, it informs the Member that it will not be published, if yes, the self-declaration is published on the OIE website (OIE, 2019[10]).[16] Publication does not imply endorsement of the claim (art. 1.6.1 *Terrestrial Code*), which is highlighted by a disclaimer on the website. It is therefore very rare that the OIE does not publish a self-declaration. If it has doubts about the veracity of a self-declaration, the OIE secretariat may suggest that the OIE Member change the nature of its self-declaration to reflect more accurately the situation in accordance with the provisions of the Codes or Manuals.

Like for official disease status, self-declarations may provide useful evidence on efforts made by OIE Members to implement OIE standards on specific diseases. In addition, the scope of self-declarations is much wider than the OIE official recognitions, as self-declarations can potentially be made for any disease with the exclusion of those diseases part of the OIE procedure for official recognition of disease status. The DSD ensures a cross-checking with WAHIS notifications to ensure consistency of information provided in self-declarations, therefore building credibility of the mechanism.

However, in practice, the assessment made by the DSD is not in-depth, and does not guarantee the scientific validity of the declaration. The responsibility of the information contained in the self-declaration lies entirely with the Delegate of the Member concerned, without guarantees from the OIE. This limits the use of these self-declarations for monitoring implementation of OIE standards.

Official Recognition of Disease Status

The OIE delivers official recognition of disease status for six diseases:

- Foot and mouth disease (FMD);
- African horse sickness (AHS);
- Classical swine fever (CSF);
- Contagious bovine pleuropneumonia (CBPP);
- Peste des petits ruminants (PPR) and
- Bovine spongiform encephalopathy (BSE) risk status.

The procedure is voluntary and is launched at the request of an OIE Member for a specific zone or an entire country, particularly when they are interested in gaining trust of export markets. OIE Members are charged a fee between 5 000 and 9 000 EUR depending on the reviewed disease. Least Developed Countries are charged a lower fee, between 2 500 and 4 500 EUR. This procedure also offers the OIE endorsement of national official control programmes for FMD, CBPP and PPR to OIE Members that may not yet have reached the level to apply for a disease-free status, but wish to apply and demonstrate its compliance with the *Terrestrial Code* provisions.

The list of OIE Members that have an official disease-free or BSE risk status is published by disease on the OIE website.[17] However, the information on the applications submitted by Members for the proposed disease status is not disclosed. For all applications submitted by Members, a detailed report is drafted on the evaluation performed by the relevant expert ad hoc Group and Specialist Commission. The assessment report on OIE Members that do not comply with OIE standards, to whom the status was not granted is kept confidential.

The majority of countries that have been recognised as free from the different diseases tend to be developed or emerging economies. For the countries who do not have the status, the information publically available is not sufficient to confirm whether this is because they have not undergone the procedure to obtain the official recognition (i.e. all countries may not have an interest in applying for disease recognition for all diseases depending on their animal exports), or because they have not received a positive assessment.

The standards that serve as a basis for the assessment of an official disease status are in the *Terrestrial Code* and *Manual*. Countries wishing to obtain the official disease status must present to the OIE Secretariat documentation demonstrating:[18]

- compliance of their veterinary services with Chapters 1.1, 3.1 and 3.2 of the *Terrestrial Code*;
- compliance with the specific criteria relating to the disease at stake. The *Terrestrial Code* includes in Chapters 1.7 – 1.12 the questionnaire countries must complete and provide documented evidence demonstrating its compliance with the provisions of the Code to achieve the disease free status for these six diseases. These chapters make reference to provisions of the relevant disease chapters in the *Terrestrial Code* and the *Terrestrial Manual*.

The information on compliance with relevant standards of the OIE *Terrestrial Code* must be substantiated in a detailed application, following the questionnaires and standard operating procedures for the official recognition of disease status.

The same procedure applies for the OIE endorsement of official control programmes, for countries who want to work towards achieving a disease-free status, but may not yet have the appropriate measures or infrastructure in place to ensure disease-free status.

The official recognition of disease status offers a rigorous procedure to assess implementation of specific OIE Standards (Box 2.4). The regular updates through the yearly reconfirmation procedure allow to have a continuous overview of the disease status in OIE Member countries. In addition, the examination of disease statuses by the OIE Secretariat provide an opportunity to ensure cross-checking of consistency between findings of PVS Evaluations and the official recognition of disease status.

Box 2.4. OIE Procedure for Official Recognition of Disease Status

The Official recognition of disease status follows a detailed procedure involving close co ordination between the OIE Secretariat, discussions by experts within an ad hoc group and examination by a Specialist Commission, the Scientific Commission for Animal Diseases (SCAD), and finally a political endorsement both by high-level management of the OIE and by the World Assembly of Delegates.

The Disease Status Department (DSD) of the OIE Secretariat is responsible for processing the applications of OIE Members for official status. This involves checking administrative and technical compliance with the *Terrestrial Code* and the rules of procedure, making sure that the OIE Member has responded to all the questions in a coherent manner.

The DSD prepares the relevant information regarding the OIE Members' application in view of its discussion in an ad hoc group, composed of experts, selected with regional representativeness and different areas of disease expertise. The ad hoc group reviews applications and may make additional questions in line with the *Terrestrial Code* requirements to the applying Member. The ad hoc group drafts a report on its assessment and formulating recommendations for SCAD, with a possible recommendation of an in country mission. Negative assessment are based on insufficient evidence provided by the assessed Member to demonstrate that the country or zone is disease-free in accordance with the *Terrestrial Code* provisions.

The application dossier and the report of the ad hoc group is then sent for examination by SCAD, who decides on the outcome of the assessment of each application. The report of SCAD meetings are made public, which includes the detailed assessment report only of countries having received a positive assessment from SCAD. Upon announcement to all OIE Delegates via an official letter informing of the OIE Members and zones for official recognition to be proposed at the General Session for adoption, other OIE Members have 60 days to ask questions about or comment on the application. In practice, some questions are posed by other Members, and the Secretariat redirects them to the assessed country. Oppositions to the proposed list of Members and zones for adoption by other Members during these 60 days happen very seldom.

The final report is endorsed by the Deputy Director General for International Standards and Science and by the Director General. Ultimately, the Official Recognition of Disease Status is recognised by the OIE World Assembly of Delegates, and adopted by a technical resolution (OIE, 2018[11]).

After the Official Status has been granted, Members must submit an application for reconfirmation by the 30th November of each year. This is to make sure that the statuses are reconfirmed annually by the OIE secretariat, to ensure that the status is up to date. The resolutions listing the OIE Members and zones having an official status or an endorsed control programme for each disease are adopted each year during the General Session.

Source: (OIE, 2019[10]), Standard Operating Procedure for official recognition of disease status and for the endorsement of national official control programmes of Member Countries, http://www.oie.int/fileadmin/home/eng/animal_health_in_the_world/docs/pdf/sop/en_sop_application.pdf.

However, to date, the process of official recognition pertains only to six diseases, which were progressively added and adopted by OIE Members to be part of this established procedure. The recourses needed to process applications for each disease are an important impediment to adding further diseases to the list.

In addition, the information on the disease free status is available publically, but mostly for the use of OIE Members in their trading relations. The OIE Secretariat does not seem to make use of official disease status for monitoring purposes. In particular, while the Secretariat has the knowledge about official disease status procedures and underlying evidence (leading to either positive or negative decision), it does not make use of this information for a general assessment on implementation of OIE standards related to these six diseases. This is in part due to a lack of resources, and in part to the will to preserve anonymity of countries who were not granted disease status.

OIE reference laboratories

The OIE provides a list of "referenced laboratories" within the *Terrestrial* and *Aquatic Manual*s, which serve as reference points for the OIE and its Member Countries on all diagnostic tests and vaccines. The endorsement process of referenced laboratories foresees the approval of the related expert with the objective to provide support to OIE Member Countries in diagnosing and controlling one specific disease (OIE, 2017[12]). These experts provide scientific and technical assistance and expert advice on all points related to the disease they are responsible for. Only one OIE Reference Laboratory per OIE Member Country for a given disease can be designated, but developed or emerging economies tend to have reference laboratories for various different diseases. France, Italy, the United Kingdom or the United States for example have more than 20 reference laboratories, and Australia, Canada, China and Germany have between 10-20 reference laboratories. A number of OIE Member countries are still lacking reference laboratories, namely in developing and least developed countries.[19]

To gain status, laboratories submit an application to the OIE following specific guidelines. The application is reviewed by the relevant Specialist Commission of the OIE (Biological Standards Commission or Aquatic Animal Health Standards Commission). The OIE Commissions assess the capacity, expertise and international reach of laboratories. In particular, they examine criteria such as the accreditation to the ISO 17025 or equivalent quality management system, the CV of the applying expert, national and international experience in diagnostic techniques, as well as capability for international shipment and receipt of samples, among others.[20] The decision of the Specialist Commission is then submitted to the OIE Council for endorsement and to the WAD for a final decision by the adoption of a technical resolution.

Reference laboratories do not as such have a mandate to monitor implementation of OIE standards. However, in the process of conducting testing or diagnoses for diseases, they obtain information about OIE Members' compliance or not with OIE standards in a specific zone or country. This information remains confidential, and may at best be communicated to the delegate of the country concerned. However, reference laboratories have an obligation to inform the OIE WAHIS team on their findings if disease outbreaks are not reported through the WAHIS system.[21] When this is the case, the OIE contacts the Member delegate to encourage an updated WAHIS notification.

Annual reports of reference laboratories do provide some information on trends in implementation of OIE standards. These reports are based on reference laboratory terms of reference, and ask a number of questions related to the use of diagnostic methods based on OIE standards by each reference laboratory. When relevant, reference laboratories provide number of tests performed in relation to OIE standards, as well as other broad information concerning the implementation of OIE Manuals.[22] While the information remains broad and in aggregates, it provides some information on the use of OIE Manuals in different regions.

In principle, a conference is held every four years between reference laboratories to promote communication and exchanges between different countries and regions. However, this conference has not been organised since 2014 due to lack of funding.

External WTO mechanisms to collect information on trade impacts of veterinary measures

The WTO has various transparency mechanisms that help provide evidence on the uptake of OIE standards. These mechanisms aim primarily to enhance the predictability and stability of measures applied by WTO Members (OECD/WTO, 2019[13]). Information shared by WTO Members through these mechanisms is centralised by the WTO Secretariat and thus made available to all WTO Members as well as to the public in general. As such, they represent an important source of information on domestic measures, including veterinary measures, with an impact on trade. Due to the encouragement for WTO Member countries to consider international standards, and in particular OIE standards, the WTO transparency mechanisms allow for some partial monitoring of the use of OIE standards in domestic veterinary measures.

WTO SPS notifications

The WTO SPS Agreement requires Members to notify domestic draft regulations when they have a significant impact on trade, when they are not based on an international standard, or that the content of the draft measure is not substantially the same as the relevant international standard (Article 7 and Annex B SPS Agreement). However, as noted above, the SPS Committee encourages notification of national measures based on international standards as well, as long as they have a significant impact on trade.

Overall, this process is an opportunity to gather evidence on the use of international standards in domestic legislation (WTO, 2009[14]) (WTO, 2008[15]). Indeed, the notification form filled in by WTO Members submitting a notification to the WTO Secretariat asks the Member to indicate the existence or not of an international standard, guideline or recommendation, whether or not the measure conforms with the international standard and if not, how and why the measure deviates from the international standard (see Annex C). The notifications submitted to the WTO contain descriptions of the measures adopted domestically, and often references to the actual texts. This information source is detailed and verifiable.

By 2018, a total of 18 277 SPS notifications had been submitted, covering areas of animal health, plant health, plant protection, food safety, etc. 23% of these notified measures indicate expressly a conformity with international standards, i.e. 4 133 SPS notifications. Out of these, 1 311 indicate conformity with OIE standards.[23] Finally, 62 SPS notifications indicate that an SPS measure is covered by an OIE standard, but the measure does not conform with it. In other words, the number of SPS notifications confirming the conformity of national measures with OIE standards is marginal when considering the broad range of domestic SPS measures. However, it is important to note that the total notifications go well beyond the area of animal health. In absolute terms, the measures conforming with OIE standards represent substantive evidence into national measures adopting an OIE standard.

However, the information obtained through SPS notifications is likely partial. In particular, WTO Members do not have the legal obligation to notify measures that comply with international standards, even though they are encouraged to do so by the SPS Committee. The obligation to notify concerns specifically measures that are not based on international standards and have a significant impact on trade. In addition, the notification form does not require WTO Members to specify the exact standard used as a basis, beyond the standard-setting body that has adopted it. This makes it difficult to track implementation of individual standards. The notifying Member can also remain broad regarding the information it discloses about the level of conformity with the international standard. WTO Members are asked to tick a box to say if yes or no their measure conforms with an international standard. This does not leave space for specifying the extent to which the national measure reproduces the international standard, or takes elements of it.

On the other hand, the notification authorities are not necessarily well trained to identify relevant international standards. Indeed, in a survey to SPS Committee Members in 2015, the major challenge to notifications identified by respondents was the difficulty to identify whether the SPS measure conformed with an international standard (WTO, 2015[16]). This may be changing however since 2015, as several OIE delegates mention coordinating on a regular basis with their country's WTO notification authority regarding domestic legislations to be notified, as well as on the interpretation of notifications by other Members.[24]

Using the WTO notifications database requires active efforts by the OIE secretariat to examine the content of the notified measures and identify its relation to OIE standards. In the first effort by OIE secretariat to make use of SPS notifications for monitoring aquatic animal health standards, (Bucher, Tellechea and Mylrea, 2019[17]) find that 77% of notifications report conforming with OIE standards. This evidence provides a useful reference to estimate compliance with OIE standards in the specific area of aquatic standards, and confirms the value of SPS notifications to monitor implementation of OIE standards. However, the authors themselves point to several limitations, including the limited number of relevant notifications (148 notifications over a period of close to 10 years), and the need to assess the notifications against the OIE standards individually, because information is not detailed by the notifying authority (Bucher, Tellechea and Mylrea, 2019, p. 7[17]).

Specific Trade Concerns raised in SPS Committee

Information publically available on WTO SPS Committee discussions represent an important source of information on the lack of implementation of international standards in general, and OIE standards in particular, as well as of the challenges and costs resulting for trading partners.

WTO Members use the SPS Committee of the WTO as a forum to discuss concerns they have with each other's measures (OECD/WTO, 2019[13]). In particular, through the procedure of Specific Trade Concerns (STCs), they highlight possible or potential inconsistencies of national measures of other Members with obligations of the SPS Agreement and the challenges or unnecessary burdens they face as a result. All STCs are documented by the WTO Secretariat on a public database, and can be freely accessed and searched.[25]

As mentioned above, the SPS Agreement includes an obligation to base SPS measures on international standards except if scientific justification or risk assessment justify a higher level of protection (art. 3.1, 3.3 SPS Agreement), and cite OIE standards as a reference for international standards on animal health (Annex A 3 (b) SPS Agreement). Therefore, the STCs, which raise possible inconsistencies with the SPS Agreement, also allow to draw attention to potential inconsistencies with OIE standards. Overall, since 1995 and by mid-2018, 128 of the 447 SPS STCs raised included a mention of the OIE in the concern (i.e. 29%). While this remains a broad aggregate, it confirms some use of this mechanism to discuss OIE-related matters in the WTO SPS Committee.

The OIE uses this data source occasionally to gather evidence on implementation of OIE standards. Most recently, the OIE Secretariat has been conducting research on trends in STCs related to avian influenza, looking into the countries that most frequently raise concern, the countries whose measures are most frequently questioned, and the types of issues that are most discussed in relation to OIE standards on avian influenza. While the research is still on going, initial findings confirm a cross-fertilization between the OIE standard-setting process and the STCs raised in the WTO (Bucher, 2017[18]).

Monitoring of the process of international harmonisation by WTO Secretariat

The SPS Agreement envisages the monitoring by the SPS Committee of international harmonization and the use of international standards, guidelines and recommendations (art. 3.5; 12.4 SPS Agreement). This procedure aims to encourage the use of international, standards and recommendations, to identify where the non-use of such standards creates a major impact on trade, and to help the relevant IOs setting the standards identify where a standard was needed or was not appropriate for its purpose or use (WTO, 2004[19]).

In virtue of this procedure, the SPS Committee monitors the process of international harmonisation at each of its regular meetings. In practice, Members use this opportunity to raise issues to the attention of the SPS Committee Members related to other Members' practice that may create barriers to trade because of a lack of consistency with international standards. These issues are then discussed in the Committee meetings and reflected in the minutes. Each year, the WTO Secretariat prepares an annual report, in which it gives an overview of the issues raised over the year (WTO, 2018[20]). Concretely, this serves as an opportunity for WTO Members to encourage compliance of other Members with international standards, including OIE standards. Box 2.5 provides examples of the OIE-related issues discussed in recent annual reports.

Box 2.5. Discussions on OIE standards in WTO SPS Committee meetings

Overview of issues in WTO SPS Committee Annual reports on the procedure to monitor the process of international harmonization:

- OIE chapter on porcine reproductive and respiratory syndrome (PRRS): noting concern that some countries were still implementing import restrictions that were not in line with OIE standards on PRRS, the United States, Canada and the European Union recalled the new OIE standard and encouraged all countries to apply the new OIE standard in this regard.[1]

- BSE Restrictions not consistent with the OIE international standard: the United States regretted numerous unjustified restrictions it faced in its exports of live bovines, bovine meat and other products, inconsistent with OIE international standards. It reiterated its commitment to aligning its import regulations governing BSE OIE Guidelines and listed the US rules that were in line with the OIE standard.[2]

- Measures on bovine semen and reproductive material more restrictive than the OIE standard: Argentina observed that Members were applying measures which were not in accordance with several articles of the OIE *Terrestrial Code*, such as Articles 8.8.15, 8.8.17 and 8.8.19.[3]

[1] June 2018 annual report, para 2.14-2.16.
[2] May 2016 annual report, para 3.13-3.14.
[3] May 2016 annual report, para. 3.18.
Source: (WTO, 2018[21]) (WTO, 2016[22]).

Trade Policy Review Mechanism[26]

WTO makes a regular monitoring of national trade policies through its Trade Policy Review Mechanism (TPRM). The purpose of the Trade Policy Review Mechanism ("TPRM") is to contribute to improved adherence by all Members to rules, disciplines and commitments made under the Multilateral Trade Agreements, including the SPS Agreement.[27] In each report, there is a specific part on "sanitary and phytosanitary measures", which provide a description of the relevant legal and institutional framework, among which the existing animal health laws and regulations and institutions involved. These reviews therefore are a useful opportunity to understand the domestic veterinary legislation frameworks. It is in this context that the requirement to base national measures on international standards in SPS measures may be addressed, among the other obligations of the SPS Agreement.

However, the reviews are prepared by the WTO Secretariat merely for transparency purposes, in close co-operation with the reviewed country. The WTO Secretariat does not have the authority to conduct an assessment of the legal consistency of domestic policies with the WTO agreements. These reviews do not incorporate systematic assessment of the use of international standards, beyond information already included in notifications to the SPS Committee or concerns raised in the SPS Committee regarding the reviewed countries' measures. Without a more detailed assessment on countries' use of international standards, this transparency mechanism does not add evidence for the purposes of the OIE Observatory.

Mechanisms to collect information and support implementation of specific thematic or regional issues

Some regional groupings have independent data collection exercises that may feed into the OIE Observatory as sources of information. This is the case, for example, of the monitoring conducted by the OIE Secretariat itself or by the EU of its Member States' measures. In addition, the OIE maintain other mechanisms specific to certain thematic issues.

OIE Mechanisms to support implementation in specific regional contexts

The OIE maintain a number of mechanisms to provide trainings on a regional basis and ensure relevance of OIE standards in different contexts. In some cases, these regional platforms are used to gather information about implementation of standards in a specific region.

Regional commissions

Regional commissions were set up at the very outsets of the OIE, in order to identify topics that were of relevance to specific regions. They are composed of representatives of countries from the same region. A "regional bureau" is elected for a mandate of three years, with four representatives of each region.[28] This bureau identifies the diseases that are of particular interest to their region, and address specific challenges that the region is facing. In addition, an informal "regional core group" creates a relation between each region and the central governance bodies of the OIE: it is composed of the four bureau Members of each given region, and of two Members of the Council from the same region. The OIE Secretariat supports regional commissions namely through its Regional Representations present in Africa, Americas, Asia and the Pacific, Europe and the Middle East.[29] However, OIE Headquarters have only a limited involvement in these activities (two Members of the OIE staff ensure coordination of activities of the five regional commissions).

Each Regional Commission organises a Conference every two years in one of their countries. These Conferences are devoted to the discussion of two technical items and to regional cooperation in the control of animal diseases.

Some regional commissions, under their own initiative, monitor the implementation of standards in their geographic area. For example, the commission for Europe set up a questionnaire to self-evaluate the control of population of stray dogs, to monitor implementation of Chapter 7.7 of the *Terrestrial Code*, and they are in the process of developing a questionnaire to evaluate implementation of Chapter 7.5 on the slaughtering of animals for human consumption. However, these monitoring initiatives depend on specific funding, and interests in given regions. And despite the rapid pace of interconnectedness that increasingly globalise regional problems, pushing the OIE regional commissions to rethink their purpose, there is so far limited co-ordination among regional commissions to disseminate the same questionnaires across regions and gather comparable evidence on implementation.

Focal point seminars

The OIE holds regional training seminars every two years (pending resources), in eight areas: animal disease notification, wildlife, veterinary products, veterinary laboratories, animal production food safety, animal welfare, aquatic animals and communication. OIE Members are invited to nominate eight national focal points specialised in each of these areas to attend the relevant seminars. One OIE staff Member is responsible for managing focal point seminars under each topic. Funding for the seminars varies considerably across regions.

The focal point seminars can be an opportunity to gather information on the Member's experience in implementing OIE standards. For example, the focal point training on Veterinary products was used as an opportunity to gather information on antimicrobial resistance related topics from focal points in all different regions. Based on the interactions with National Focal Points, the template of questions for the yearly OIE General survey on antimicrobial agents intended for use in animals was finalised. There is not, however, a centralised approach to gathering information on the implementation of existing standards, as the objective of most seminars is to provide updates on revised or newly developed standards, encourage participation in the standard-setting process, and build networks in line with the Terms of reference for each Focal Point topic.

EU monitoring of EU Member States' measures

The monitoring of EU Member states' measures allows for a comprehensive monitoring of existing animal health and disease legislation and practice. This monitoring of conformity with EU legislation is particularly interesting because all information is made available to the public online. In particular, the European Commission develops detailed "country profiles" for each EU Member State on issues of food and food safety, animal health, animal welfare and plant health. Concretely, these are individual pages on the EC website, containing the following information:[30]

- The five most recently published audit reports by the DG Health and Food Safety in all areas related to health and food, including related to animal health. Member states are expected to present action plans for addressing the shortcomings revealed in these audits;
- The EC assessment of the actions taken by the Member states in response to its audits and audit recommendations, in relation to the action plans set by the Member States. This assessment is presented in the form of a report prepared by DG Health and Food Safety;
- An overview of how controls are organised in the Member states, based on information supplied by them;
- Relevant links to Member states' websites, providing access to official domestic documentation, including when available, the annual reports on implementation of the action plans to address Commission audit recommendations.

These country profiles provide information on Member-state legislation in relation to EU legislation, rather than directly in relation to OIE standards. In addition, these country profiles go beyond the sphere of animal health. However, all components of the country profile listed above contain a section on animal health, including when relevant references to the legal and institutional framework related to implementing OIE standards. Therefore, the thoroughness of the information gathered and the assessment made by the EC in this regard include detailed evidence that may help build better understanding on implementation of OIE standards.

Mechanisms to monitor implementation on specific thematic issues

The OIE Member countries may choose to put a specific emphasis on certain thematic issues, therefore highlighting implementation of the existing OIE standards in this area. This may be done for example via thematic items raised in the yearly World Assembly of Delegates, or in a more ad hoc manner when there is demand on specific issues.

Monitoring of implementation through technical items at the World Assembly of Delegates (WAD)

The OIE WAD is an opportunity to launch discussions about priority topics high on the international agenda with the entire OIE Membership. Two technical items are raised at most annual WAD meetings:

- One of the technical items is based on the results of a questionnaire developed by experts, and responded by OIE Members. The theme of this technical item is defined at the General Assembly among all regional commissions, in a four-hour session dedicated to identifying such themes, based on proposals by regional Core groups.
- The second technical item is decided in the meeting of the OIE Council in February. To develop analytical work for this technical item, experts may be chosen, namely from the pool of experts of the Collaborating Centres.

While noting survey fatigue among Member Countries, the technical item involving a questionnaire may offer a particularly useful avenue to gather information on implementation of OIE standards. Indeed, as the questionnaires result in an analytical report discussed in the WAD annual meeting, there is strong incentive for Members to respond to the questionnaire making their coverage close to exhaustive. The results of the technical item questionnaires are made publically available in aggregates, but not at the country-level.

A telling example is the questionnaire developed in 2017-18, the results of which were presented at the 86th General Session in May 2018. This questionnaire aimed to gather an overview on the implementation of OIE standards by OIE Member countries in the context of international trade. The responses allow to understand the general approaches OIE Members take to implementation of OIE standards: in particular, the respondents indicate how systematic the consideration of international standards is for them, what sort of procedures are in place to consider international standards, and which OIE normative instruments are mostly used. The results were analysed in a Secretariat paper (Kahn, 2018[23]) and have been synthesised for the purposed of this note in Chapter 3, Annex A.

Monitoring of implementation of certain standards related to anti-microbial resistance (AMR)

AMR is a phenomenon that applies to human, animal and plant health. Therefore, specific procedures have been put in place to monitor antimicrobial resistance, jointly managed by the WHO, OIE and the FAO. In response to interests raised in different international *fora* (WHO, FAO, OIE), the OIE has been conducting specific monitoring on its standards related to AMR, in particular the use of antimicrobial agents in animals.

The OIE has the following standards applicable on the issue:

- Terrestrial Animal Health Code (Chapters 6.7, 6.8, 6.9, 6.10 and 6.11).
- Manual of Diagnostic Tests and Vaccines for Terrestrial Animals (Chapter 3.1).
- Aquatic Animals Health Code (Chapters 6.1, 6.2, 6.3, 6.4 and 6.5).

In addition, the OIE has a specific strategy on antimicrobial resistance in veterinary products (OIE, 2016[24]), and has developed a list of antimicrobial agents of veterinary importance (OIE, 2018[25]).

OIE general survey on antimicrobial agents intended for use in animals

Two specific recommendations of the OIE World Assembly suggested further development of OIE standards related to AMR and to enhance the support for their adoption at the national level:[31]

> *"3. The OIE develop a procedure and standards for data quality for collecting data annually from OIE Member Countries on the use of antimicrobial agents in food-producing animals with the aim of creating an OIE global database to be managed in parallel with the World Animal Health Information System (WAHIS)."*
>
> *"4. OIE Member Countries set up an official harmonised national system, based on OIE standards, for the surveillance of antimicrobial resistance and the collection of data on the use of antimicrobial agents in food-producing animals, and actively participate in the development of the OIE global database."*

Against this impetus, an OIE ad hoc Group on antimicrobial resistance has developed a template for harmonised data collection, and guidance for completing the template.[32] The template provides an overview of how many Countries have responded and the level of details that can be provided by each country. When processing responses, the Secretariat uses data from WAHIS to cross-check the responses received through the template. This data collection entails the monitoring of the quantities of antimicrobial agents used as required in Chapter 6.8 of the *Terrestrial Code* and Chapter 6.3 of the *Aquatic Code*. The results of the monitoring are presented in an Annual Report prepared by the OIE. The results are aggregates at the global and regional levels, not by individual country.

The AMR studies provide for a significant tool to gather evidence on the country practices related to antimicrobial resistance, falling under standards of the OIE *Terrestrial* and *Aquatic Code*s.

Global monitoring of country progress on addressing antimicrobial resistance

The OIE, FAO and WHO Members agreed to a joint Action Plan on AMR in 2015. Among others, countries committed to develop AMR national action plans on the status of AMR in their country. The three organisations monitor the implementation of these national action plans by countries. The monitoring is done via a self-assessment survey prepared by the three organisations, with questions on AMR in plant, animal and human health.[33] The questions on animal health make references to specific OIE standards, with links to the right standard (Box 2.6).

The first two rounds of monitoring are available online, by country.[34] Some specific survey questions developed by the OIE allow to assess implementation of OIE standards, as explicit links to the relevant OIE standards are included in the questionnaire. In addition, the co-ordination among the OIE, FAO and the WHO provides an interesting example of joint data collection on monitoring of standards on a horizontal concern for several organisations.

As this exercise remains limited to three OIE standards, the value of the evidence for the purposes of the OIE Observatory remain limited. In addition, the responses provided by responding countries are very brief, and do not provide evidence on the instruments adopted to implement OIE standards. Finally, the information gathered relies merely on a self-assessment. There is therefore no quality-check by the OIE secretariat on the actual implementation of the relevant OIE standards.

Box 2.6. Survey questions with specific references to OIE standards

		6.6 Progress with strengthening veterinary services
O	A	No systematic approach at national level to strengthening Veterinary Services.
O	B	Veterinary services assessed and plans developed to improve capacity, through a structured approach such as OIE Performance of Veterinary Services (PVS) Evaluation and PVS Analysis missions.
O	C	Implementation of plan to strengthen capacity gaps in Veterinary Services underway.
O	D	Monitoring of Veterinary Services performance carried out regularly, e.g., through PVS Evaluation Follow Up missions.
O	E	Documented evidence of strong capacity in compliance with OIE standards on the quality of Veterinary Services.[1]

[1] http://www.oie.int/index.php?id=169&L=0&htmfile=chapitre_vet_serv.htm, Chapter 3.1: "Terrestrial Animal Health Code".

		7.2 National monitoring system for antimicrobials intended to be used in animals (sales/use)
O	A	No national plan or system for monitoring sales/use of antimicrobials in animals.
O	B	Plan agreed for monitoring quantities of antimicrobials sold for /used in animals, based on OIE standards.[1]
O	C	Data collected and reported on total quantity of AMs sold for /used in animals and their intended type of use (therapeutic or growth promotion)
O	D	Ono a regular basic, data is collected and reported to the OIE on the total quantity of antimicrobials sold for/used in animals nationally, by antimicrobial class, by species (aquatic or terrestrial), method of administration, and by type of use (therapeutic or growth promotion)
O	E	Data on antimicrobials used under veterinary supervision in animals are available at farm level, for individual animal species.

[1] www.oie.int/index.php?id=169&L=0&htmfile=chapitre_antibio_monitoring.htm, Chapter 6.9: "Terrestrial Animal Health Code"; www.oie.int/index.php?id=171&L=0&htmfile=chapitre_antibio_quantities_usage_patterns.htm, Chapter 6.3: "Aquatic Animal Health Code".

Conclusion: Key features of existing mechanisms supporting and monitoring the implementation of OIE standards

A number of internal and external sources of information on country activity in the OIE areas exist, providing a wealth of information upon which the Observatory may tap. These focus almost exclusively on the OIE Codes, and to a more limited extent on OIE Manuals. Country coverage may also differ, depending on the type and objective of the monitoring mechanisms (capacity building vs. transparency for regulatory and trade purposes). The level of the collected information is often the country, although aggregates may be produced. Availability may be subject to country decision.

The mechanisms that have been set up at the OIE to collect data are not primarily directed at monitoring implementation of OIE standards. They nevertheless provide useful information on the implementation of OIE standards at the domestic level, as a collateral of their own objectives. The OIE gathers a mix of input, output and outcome data that may lead to analytical work and assessment to understand the impact of OIE standards.

However, because the objective is not a systematic monitoring of implementation, the information gathered does not necessarily cover all OIE Members or is not directly of interest to such exercise. For example, the country coverage of the most in-depth OIE mechanisms (the PVS) is limited to countries that make a request and has been mostly undertaken by developing countries, owing to its capacity building rationale.

By contrast, the official recognition of disease status has largely focused on developed and emerging countries who have exporting interests. In theory, the detailed scrutiny involved in such recognition may be applied to any OIE Member. In practice, however, the limitation of information to positive disease statuses, combined with the need for substantial resources to conduct the process, have constrained the scope of the mechanism.

Overall, a number of OIE mechanisms may still be tapped into further, in order to obtain more comprehensive evidence on implementation of OIE standards. This is for example the case for the Thematic Items of the World Assembly of Delegates, which take place systematically every year and receive visibility from the entire OIE Membership; focal points seminars may be also an opportunity to gather information on the Members' experience in implementing OIE standards.

Mechanisms used in other IOs complement the evidence gathered today by OIE mechanisms and may also be used more systematically to complement OIE own mechanisms. This is particularly the case with monitoring conducted by the EU, in a particularly thorough manner for its Member States. In addition, the transparency mechanisms of the WTO may offer an avenue to find out about national measures, which adopt or not OIE standards.

Notes

[1] Data based on information provided by the OIE Secretariat, listing the standards monitored by existing monitoring mechanisms, against a basis of 389 Chapters of 2018 version of the OIE Terrestrial and *Aquatic Code*s and Manuals (*Terrestrial Code* - TC (147), *Terrestrial Manual* - TM (137), *Aquatic Code* – AC (65), *Aquatic Manual* – AM (40)). See Annex B.

[2] "Veterinary services means the governmental and non-governmental organisations that implement animal health and welfare measures and other standards and recommendations in the *Terrestrial Code* and the OIE Aquatic Animal Health Code in the territory. The Veterinary Services are under the overall control and direction of the Veterinary Authority. Private sector organisations, veterinarians, veterinary paraprofessionals or aquatic animal health professionals are normally accredited or approved by the Veterinary Authority to deliver the delegated functions." OIE Glossary, www.oie.int/index.php?id=169&L=0&htmfile=glossaire.htm#terme_services_veterinaires.

[3] www.oie.int/index.php?id=169&L=0&htmfile=titre_1.3.htm.

[4] www.oie.int/index.php?id=171&L=0&htmfile=titre_1.3.htm.

[5] www.oie.int/en/solidarity/pvs-evaluations/status-of-missions/.

[6] Their reports are available at www.oie.int/en/solidarity/pvs-evaluations/pvs-evaluation-reports/.

[7] See PVS Evaluation Report of Canada, p. 5.
www.oie.int/fileadmin/Home/eng/Support_to_OIE_Members/docs/pdf/201804_09_final_OIE_PVS_Evaluation_report_Canada_Eng.pdf.

[8] See for e.g. p. 7 in OIE PVS Evaluation Follow-up Mission Report of Turkey, 2017, p. 7.
www.oie.int/fileadmin/Home/eng/Support_to_OIE_Members/docs/pdf/20180307_final_OIE_PVS_FU_report_Turkey.pdf.

[9] www.oie.int/en/solidarity/veterinary-legislation/status-of-missions/.

[10] www.fao.org/faolex/en/.

[11] http://oie.int/fileadmin/pdfs/Overview_of_the_VLSP_Electronic_version.pdf.

[12] www.oie.int/wahis_2/public/wahid.php/Wahidhome/Home/index/newlang/en.

[13] www.oie.int/en/for-the-media/press-releases/detail/article/oie-alerts-and-animal-health-information-now-available-on-your-smartphone-or-tablet/.

[14] There is a reference to Chapter 1.1 (notification of disease) and for two diseases control and prevention measures ("compartmentalisation" and "stamping out"); for the other measures, there is no reference.

[15] www.oie.int/animal-health-in-the-world/self-declared-disease-status/.

[16] Until 2017, the publication of self-declarations was done in a bulletin issued four times a year, and self-declarations had to be submitted at specific dates to be published in time. Today, the publication of self-declaration is done online, therefore in a more transparent and timely manner. See list of self-declarations: www.oie.int/en/animal-health-in-the-world/self-declared-disease-status/.

[17] www.oie.int/en/animal-health-in-the-world/official-disease-status/.

[18] See art 1.6.1 *Terrestrial Code*.

[19] For overview of world distribution of reference laboratories, see www.oie.int/en/scientific-expertise/reference-laboratories/map-and-networks/.

[20] For full set of criteria, see Guidelines for applicants for OIE Reference Laboratory Status, at www.oie.int/en/our-scientific-expertise/reference-laboratories/guidelines-for-applicants/.

[21] See Article 2 of Intern Rules of OIE Reference Laboratories, https://www.oie.int/en/scientific-expertise/reference-laboratories/criteria-and-internal-rules/.

[22] See for example OIE Reference Laboratory Reports Activities, 2017, United Kingdom, for African horse sickness www.oie.int/fileadmin/home/eng/our_scientific_expertise/reflabreports/2017/report_312_2017_african_horse_sickness_united_kingdom.pdf; or OIE Reference Laboratory Reports Activities, 2017, South Africa www.oie.int/fileadmin/home/eng/our_scientific_expertise/reflabreports/2017/report_390_2017_african_horse_sickness_south_africa.pdf.

[23] Information gathered on http://spsims.wto.org/. This figure accounts only for regular and emergency notifications submitted between 1 January 1995 and 31 December 2018, without counting addenda, corrigenda and revisions to the original notification.

[24] Interviews conducted by OECD with OIE delegates for the purpose of this study.

[25] The specific trade concerns raised in the SPS Committee are searchable here: http://spsims.wto.org/en/SpecificTradeConcerns/Search.

[26] www.wto.org/english/tratop_e/tpr_e/tpr_e.htm.

[27] Annex 3 of Agreement Establishing the WTO, Para A.

[28] List of bureau Members: www.oie.int/about-us/wo/oie-regional-commissions/.

[29] www.oie.int/about-us/wo/oie-regional-representations/.

[30] http://ec.europa.eu/food/audits-analysis/country_profiles/index.cfm.

[31] OIE World Assembly of Delegates in 2015 in Resolution No. 26, "Combating Antimicrobial Resistance and Promoting the Prudent Use of Antimicrobial Agents in Animals", www.oie.int/fileadmin/Home/eng/Our_scientific_expertise/docs/pdf/amr/a_reso_amr_2015.pdf.

[32] Both are available in annexes of OIE Annual Report on the use of antimicrobial agents in animals. www.oie.int/fileadmin/Home/eng/Our_scientific_expertise/docs/pdf/AMR/Survey_on_monitoring_antimicrobial_agents_Dec2016.pdf and www.oie.int/fileadmin/Home/eng/Our_scientific_expertise/docs/pdf/AMR/Annual_Report_AMR_2.pdf.

33 www.who.int/antimicrobial-resistance/global-action-plan/AMR-self-assessment-country-questionnaire-2017-English.pdf?ua=1.

34 https://amrcountryprogress.org/.

References

Bucher, K. (2017), *Analysis of the AI-related trade concerns raised by Member Countries*. [18]

Bucher, K., D. Tellechea and G. Mylrea (2019), "Safe trade of aquatic animals and aquatic animal products: exploring the use of OIE international standards for setting sanitary measures", *OIE Scientific and Technical Review*, Vol. 38/2. [17]

Eurostat (2014), *Getting messages across using indicators: A handbook based on experiences from assessing Sustainable Development Indicators*, Publications Office of the European Union. [7]

Kahn, B. (2018), *Implementation of OIE Standards by OIE Member Countries: State of Play and Specific Capacity Building Needs. Descriptive Analysis of the Questionnaire*. [23]

OECD (2019), *Open Government in Biscay*, OECD Public Governance Reviews, OECD Publishing, Paris, https://dx.doi.org/10.1787/e4e1a40c-en. [1]

OECD (2018), *OECD Regulatory Policy Outlook 2018*, OECD Publishing, Paris, https://dx.doi.org/10.1787/9789264303072-en. [4]

OECD (2017), *Towards Open Government Indicators: Framework for the Governance of Open Government (GOOG) Index and the Checklist for Open Government Impact Indicators*, OECD Publishing. [3]

OECD (2016), *International Regulatory Co-operation: The Role of International Organisations*, OECD Publishing. [5]

OECD (2016), *The monitoring and evaluation of open government strategies and practices, in Open Government: The Global Context and the Way Forward*, OECD Publishing. [2]

OECD (2010), *Glossary of Key Terms in Evaluation and Results Based Management*. [6]

OECD/WTO (2019), *Facilitating Trade through Regulatory Cooperation: The Case of the WTO's TBT/SPS Agreements and Committees*, OECD Publishing, Paris/World Trade Organization, Geneva, https://dx.doi.org/10.1787/ad3c655f-en. [13]

OIE (2019), *OIE Tool for the Evaluation of Performance of Veterinary Services, PVS Tool, Seventh Edition*, http://www.oie.int/fileadmin/Home/eng/Support_to_OIE_Members/pdf/AF-PVSTool.pdf. [8]

OIE (2019), *Standard Operating Procedure on the publication of the self-declaration of freedom from diseases of Members Codes: Terrestrial Animal Health Code and Aquatic Animal Health Code, A-Submission of Self-Declarations by Members (Section A of Guidelines)*, http://www.oie.int/fileadmin/Home/eng/Animal_Health_in_the_World/docs/pdf/Self-declarations/EN_Procedure_self_declaration.pdf (accessed on 6 November 2018).   [10]

OIE (2018), *OIE List of Antimicrobial Agents of Veterinary Importance*, http://www.oie.int/fileadmin/Home/eng/Our_scientific_expertise/docs/pdf/AMR/A_OIE_List_antimicrobials_May2018.pdf.   [25]

OIE (2018), *Standard Operating Procedure for official recognition of disease status and for the endorsement of national official control programmes of Member Countries*, http://www.oie.int/fileadmin/Home/eng/Animal_Health_in_the_World/docs/pdf/SOP/EN_SOP_Application.pdf (accessed on 6 November 2018).   [11]

OIE (2017), *Procedures for designation of OIE Reference Laboratories*, http://www.oie.int/en/our-scientific- (accessed on 15 November 2018).   [12]

OIE (2016), *The OIE Strategy on Antimicrobial Resistance and the Prudent Use of Antimicrobials*, http://www.oie.int/fileadmin/Home/eng/Media_Center/docs/pdf/PortailAMR/EN_OIE-AMRstrategy.pdf.   [24]

OIE (2013), *OIE Tool for the Evaluation of Performance of Veterinary Services, PVS Tool, Sixth Edition*, http://www.oie.int/fileadmin/Home/eng/Support_to_OIE_Members/pdf/PVS_A_Tool_Final_Edition_2013.pdf.   [9]

WTO (2018), *Annual Report on the Procedure to Monitor the Process of International Harmonization*.   [21]

WTO (2018), *Annual Report on the Procedure to Monitor the Process of International Harmonization, Note by the Secretariat*.   [20]

WTO (2016), *Annual Report on the Procedure to Monitor the Process of International Harmonization*.   [22]

WTO (2015), *Questionnaire on Transparency under the SPS Agreement*, G/SPS/GEN/1382.   [16]

WTO (2009), *Fifth Triennial Review of the Operation and Implementation of the Agreement on Technical Barriers to Trade Under Article 15.4 G/TBT/26*.   [14]

WTO (2008), *Recommended Procedures for Implementing the Transparency Obligation of the SPS Agreement (Article 7), G/SPS/7/Rev.2*.   [15]

WTO (2004), *Revision of the procedure to monitor the process of international harmonization*.   [19]

3 Recommendations for the establishment of the OIE Observatory

This chapter provides recommendations to support the establishment of the OIE Observatory on Standards Implementation. These recommendations build on the specificities of OIE standards, the institutional framework of the OIE, and the existing information collection mechanisms as reflected in previous chapters, as well as on a comparative analysis of selected IO experiences.

The OIE has embarked on an ambitious and unique exercise with the establishment of the OIE Observatory. In May 2018, the World Assembly of OIE Delegates adopted the Resolution No. 36 recommending the creation of an Observatory on the implementation of OIE Standards by Member Countries. Subsequently, the OIE put in place a specific governance to carry out the project and called on the OECD to support this undertaking building on work done with 50 international organisations (IOs) on the quality of international rulemaking.[1] This preparatory work has laid the ground for a thorough reflection on the critical objectives, modalities and challenges of OIE standard-setting and the opportunities for better monitoring of implementation at domestic level.

To make the most out of this opportunity, the design of the Observatory should reflect the specific objectives and traits of the OIE standard implementation and build on the existing practices and strengths of the organisation as reflected in this report. In particular, OIE standards aim to ensure transparency around animal health status, build good governance of veterinary services and support safe trade of animals and animal products. These standards are expert-driven and voluntary. Their voluntary nature reflects the need to account for specific country conditions (diseases are not present everywhere, diversity in production and trade profiles) and for implementation modalities that fit different regulatory systems. The implementation of OIE standards is a key responsibility of OIE members, with support from the Headquarters through guidance and capacity building. Members are incentivised to adopt OIE standards in national legislation, including through explicit promotion of OIE standards in the WTO SPS Agreement. While a thorough monitoring of the implementation of OIE standards is not yet in place, a number of information collection mechanisms, whether internal to the OIE or external, already give indication on their use in a range of Member countries and provide solid starting points for the future monitoring mechanisms.

It is noteworthy that while most IOs offer their constituency some forms of assistance for the implementation of their normative instruments, only a few have established an actual "Observatory", and none of the similar initiatives equate to the level of ambition set for the OIE Observatory. IO support generally takes the form of training programmes or implementation tools / guides. In some cases, the IOs also track the implementation of their instruments (OECD, 2016[1]). However, the IO mechanisms to monitor implementation tend to relate to legally binding instruments, for example in the field of human rights, rather than voluntary standards. They also tend to monitor the field of the IO at large rather than the implementation of the legal instruments more narrowly. Therefore, no other IO monitoring mechanism can be used as an exact model for the future OIE Observatory. Nevertheless, many IOs have established mechanisms to "observe" realities under their mandate and collect information on national systems in their field of activity. Specific lessons can be drawn from these various experiences and serve loosely as an inspiration for the establishment of the Observatory.

Building on the key features of OIE standard implementation and data collection described in previous chapters, as well as on a comparative analysis of selected IO experiences, this section offers recommendations to the OIE in support of the establishment of its Observatory. These recommendations aim to account for the specific nature of OIE standards and leverage the existing information collection mechanisms on OIE standards, while learning from other monitoring experiences. They are organised in three parts (and summarised in Box 3.1): i) the objectives and rationale for the establishment of the Observatory; ii) the scope of the future Observatory's activities; and iii) considerations on the modalities of the future "Observatory".

Setting the objectives of the OIE Observatory

In 2018, the OIE General Assembly identified a number of objectives associated with the establishment of the Observatory, emphasising 1) the importance of identifying OIE Members' assistance needs; as well as 2) improving the quality and relevance of OIE standards:

> *The OIE develop an Observatory to monitor the implementation of its international standards, to increase transparency and to identify constraints and difficulties faced by Member Countries. The design of the Observatory should ensure an efficient and integrated collection, analysis and reporting of information on progress and challenges associated with implementation of OIE international standards by Member Countries in a manner that incentivises increasing harmonisation while maintaining anonymity of the Member Countries;*
>
> *In addition to monitoring the implementation of the international standards, the Observatory should evaluate the relevance, feasibility and effectiveness of the standards to Member Countries, as a basis to develop a more strategic focus to the OIE standard setting and capacity building work programmes.[2]*

In this sense, the OIE is in line with international practice. Overall, out of 36 IOs surveyed by the OECD in 2018 (OECD, 2019[2]), the majority of IO Secretariats conduct active data collection from publicly available sources, questionnaires, or on-site missions, or rely on voluntary reporting of information on implementation by their Members. The information collected by IOs is used to assess the overall or the individual implementation of instruments. It feeds in compliance or capacity building programmes. It supports self-reflection on the defects in instruments and the need for their revision and serves to promote the use of the instruments. IOs may combine many of the above objectives. However, IOs more rarely use the information for enforcement purposes or for evaluating the performance of instruments, in particular for assessing whether or not they achieve their objectives (Figure 3.1). This owes largely to the mostly voluntary nature of international instruments and to the lack of granular data on specific member's implementation. Limited evaluation of international instruments also underlines one of the shortcomings of international rulemaking that the OECD Partnership for Effective International Rulemaking (IO Partnership) aims to address.

Figure 3.1. For what purpose is information on implementation used by international organisations?

36 respondents

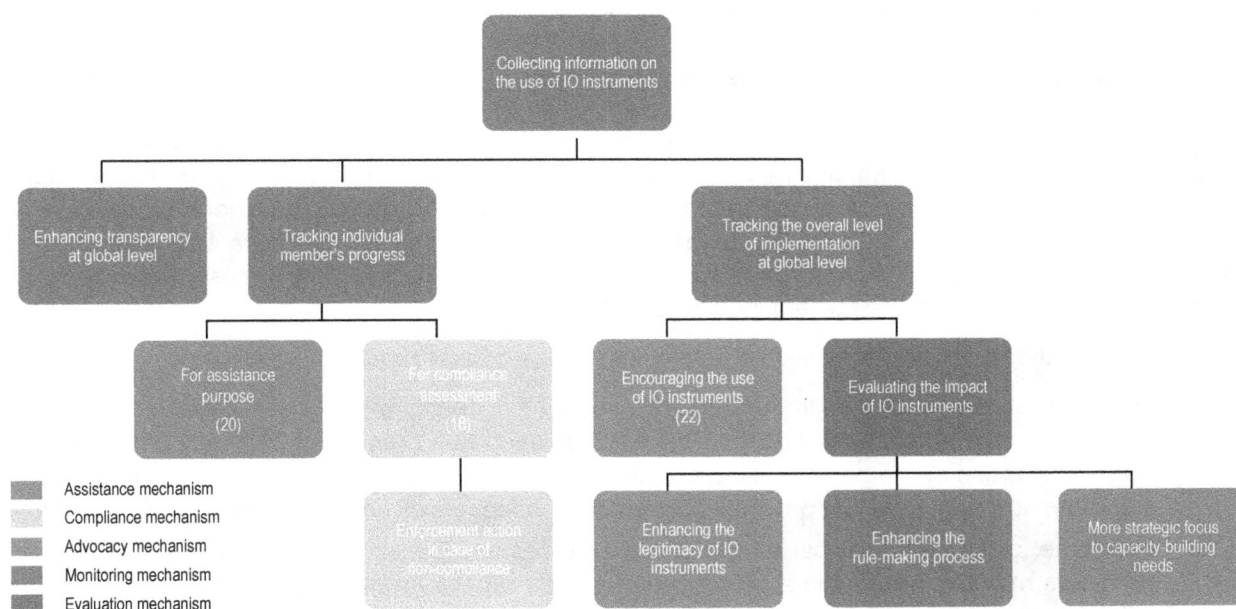

Note: The figures in brackets reflect the number of IOs reporting such mechanisms.
Source: (OECD, 2019[2]), *The Contribution of International Organisations to a Rule-Based International System*, Paris, http://www.oecd.org/gov/regulatory-policy/IO-Rule-Based%20System.pdf.

Given the nature of OIE standards and existing data collection mechanisms, the Observatory could focus on two interrelated objectives of its monitoring activity: 1) Identifying Members' capacity assistance needs and successful practices in implementing OIE standards; and 2) Enhancing the standard-setting process through evidence-based assessments of the actual use of OIE standards. These two complementary objectives are detailed below. A more compliance-focused approach aiming to enforce OIE standards would be difficult given the voluntary nature of OIE standards, and the flexibility allowed in their implementation.

Monitoring implementation to identify Members' assistance needs and successful practices

The OIE already relies on a number of mechanisms to identify the capacity building needs of members. For example, the PVS framework is a complex system of evaluation of the quality of veterinary services, which results notably in assisting evaluated countries in the reinforcement of their veterinary services.

Building on the broader monitoring that it will carry out, the OIE Observatory could aim to systematically identify technical assistance needs on a broader scope, beyond veterinary services. By identifying Members who struggle to implement certain standards, or specific areas of the Codes and Manuals that receive less attention from countries, the OIE Observatory will provide relevant information to target both Secretariat and donors' assistance activities and support the relevant departments in their efforts to tailor capacity building initiatives.

Beyond the more systematic identification of challenges and related capacity building needs, the Observatory will be in a unique position to monitor Members' practices in implementing OIE standards over time. The gathered information could help other jurisdictions struggling in their own application of OIE standards by highlighting ways, including new ones, of implementing the body of OIE instruments. This aspect of the monitoring exercise offers the OIE Observatory a broader scope of action of relevance to all its Members and enables a powerful peer learning exercise. It also allows for a dynamic use of the Observatory as implementation practices are likely to evolve over time.

Monitoring implementation to strengthen the quality and relevance of OIE standards

Using the monitoring of implementation to improve the quality and relevance of international standards is an ambitious objective, which remains rarely pursued by IOs on a systematic basis. The OIE Observatory could help achieve this objective, using information collected by the existing mechanisms to identify strengths and weaknesses in the OIE standards' use and application. The data collected by the Observatory over time could be gathered into a database and would help identify trends, challenges and gaps in implementation to feed back into the OIE standard-setting process.

The OIE standard-setting process would be enhanced in three different ways:

- The information collected by the Observatory could help identify whether specific standards have unintended consequences or ancillary impacts that need to be remedied. It is only after their full adoption and use by Members that the extent of the impacts of international standards materialise. Therefore, it is only then that potential unintended consequences can be identified and corrected.

- Over time, given technological progress and changes in production and consumption patterns, standards may become outdated and obsolete. Their regular monitoring is a critical condition to assess their continued relevance and to signal a need for their revision. It is also an essential baseline exercise to assess the need for and motivate the development of new standards.

- Finally, given the wide range of information collected by the OIE – pertaining to the use of standards, the state of domestic veterinary and animal health legislation, disease outbreaks and trade flows and concerns – the Observatory is in a good position to go beyond a mere data collection platform and draw analysis linking standards and outcomes in the field. Beyond monitoring the use of OIE standards, this analysis would open the door for a better understanding of their effectiveness at influencing outcomes (i.e. quality of veterinary services, improving animal health and welfare, and facilitating safe international trade).

Ultimately, the capacity of the Observatory to influence OIE standards will depend on the feedback loops with the standard-setting process, in particular its connection with the Specialist Commissions, so that the former informs the latter when there is a need to reconsider a standard or to develop a new one.

While experience with observatories is scarce among IOs, a number of them have developed systematic mechanisms to review the implementation of their standards and identify the improvements needed to enhance their effectiveness. This is the case of the International Organization for Standardisation (ISO), which conducts systematic reviews of all of its standards every five years maximum to identify their use and deduce their relevance and effectiveness (Box 3.1). The IPPC is currently in the process of introducing a monitoring and evaluation mechanism aimed at improving effectiveness, involving indicators on standard-setting, implementation and on integration and support. These examples provide interesting evaluation practices that could inspire the OIE in a future stage of the Observatory to connect information collection and evaluation and revision of standards.

Box 3.1. Systematic reviews in International Organization for Standardization (ISO)

The ISO has a systematic review process that can be initiated by a technical committee, a national standardisation body, by the ISO/CS or by the ISO Secretariat.

Table 3.1 shows the maximum time that can elapse before a systematic review takes place, but committees can choose to launch a review much earlier, if they believe it necessary.

Table 3.1. Timing of ISO systematic reviews

Deliverable	Max. elapsed time before systematic review	Max. number of times deliverable may be confirmed	Max. life
International standard	5 years	Not limited	Not limited
Technical specification	3 years	Once recommended	6 years recommended
Publicly available specification	3 years — no default action by ISO Central Secretariat	Once	6 years (If not converted after this period, the deliverable is proposed for withdrawal)
Technical report	Not specified	Not specified	Not limited

Source: ISO/IEC Directives Part 1. See also (OECD/ISO, 2016[3]).

Defining the scope of the OIE Observatory

On the one hand, the OIE Observatory should aim to serve the core objectives of the OIE, namely: i) foster transparency on the sanitary status of animal diseases for country, zone or compartment; ii) build good governance of the national animal health and welfare systems through improved legal frameworks and resources of veterinary services; and iii) support world trade in animals and animal products by ensuring safe international trade, while avoiding unjustified sanitary barriers to trade. This mandate provides a broad scope of potential activity for the Observatory. The Recommendation by the World Assembly of Delegates explicitly states that the OIE Observatory's activities should include an integrated collection of information, an analysis of the information collected and a reporting of information on the progress and challenges associated with implementation.

On the other hand, taking into account resource constraints and the need for a gradual approach that allows for learning by doing, the OIE Observatory should start by focusing on selected instruments and existing sources of information to help channel its resources and test its activity. This calls for a prioritisation of the OIE standards that will be the focus of the Observatory (before progressive expansion) and for a practical approach to the concept of implementation.

Normative scope of OIE Observatory: initial focus on monitoring of Terrestrial and Aquatic Codes, the basis of OIE normative work

As underlined throughout the study and summarised in Table 3.2, the *Terrestrial* and *Aquatic Codes* and Manuals are the most substantive OIE instruments of external normative value (i.e. addressed to Members and not the Secretariat itself), and serve as a basis for the other instruments developed by the organisation. They follow an in-depth and evidence-based development process, and are the subject of most of the information collection exercises in place to date. Therefore, they offer a logical starting point for the monitoring activities of the Observatory. However, even the Manuals themselves can be considered as deriving from the Codes, in that they aim to provide a uniform approach to the detection of diseases listed in the Codes. The OIE Observatory could therefore start by focusing on monitoring the implementation of the Codes, before broadening its scope.

Table 3.2. Overview of OIE instruments, addressees, bodies involved and related monitoring mechanisms

OIE name	Addressees	Body/ authority involved in development	Monitoring mechanism
Codes	OIE Members	Specialist commissions; permanent working groups; ad hoc groups; WAD	PVS Pathway; WAHIS; Official recognition of disease status; self-declarations; Anti-microbial resistance Global study
Manuals	OIE Members	Specialist commissions; permanent working groups; ad hoc groups; WAD	Official recognition of disease status; Reference laboratories
Technical resolution	OIE Members OIE Secretariat	WAD	N/A
Administrative resolution	OIE Secretariat	WAD	N/A
Recommendations of Regional Commissions	OIE Members OIE Secretariat	Regional Commissions; WAD	N/A
Recommendations of Global Conference	OIE Members OIE Secretariat	Global Conference	N/A
Guidelines, checklists, etc.	OIE Members	Expert; OIE Secretariat	N/A
Code of Conduct	OIE Secretariat staff	OIE Secretariat	N/A
MoUs, co-operation agreements	OIE Secretariat, other international organisations	OIE Secretariat	N/A

Source: Author's own elaboration based on OIE responses to OECD 2018 survey to international organisations.

Still, the *Terrestrial* and *Aquatic Codes* together represent around 212 chapters, all of which include several articles. Therefore, even narrowing these efforts to the Codes, prioritisation remains important, particularly in the early stages of establishing the Observatory, in order to allow for a piloting phase. The very first step for the OIE Observatory would be to deepen the work initiated in Annex B to map the OIE standards (or the parts) that are already the object of data collection under the existing OIE mechanisms as summarised in Table 3.3 (PVS or other).

Annex B provides a starting point but would need a more granular analysis of the links between the data currently collected by the OIE and others and the standards covered. This mapping exercise could help clarify the scope of information already collected, the current gaps, the easy extensions and the analytical needs where raw data would not achieve the purpose of the monitoring. In particular, the mapping should seek to identify: the connection with the underlying OIE standards; the geographic coverage; the frequency of the collected information (ad hoc or regular and if so how often); the nature of information (quantitative, qualitative); the level of availability of the information (public or limited) and the level of the validation (self-reporting versus quality check carried out by the OIE).

Subsequently, the OIE Observatory may extend its monitoring scope to a broader set of standards, while still prioritizing those that are of most importance for achieving the objectives of the OIE. To identify these standards, the organisation could survey its Members to gather their priorities and areas of key interest. For example, it may choose to focus on standards with a broad scope of application, i.e. that concern OIE Members at large, independent of their level of development and of geographic specificities.

Material scope of OIE Observatory: broad and flexible understanding of the concept of implementation

Given the nature of OIE standards, the concept of implementation will remain elusive and cover different realities in various jurisdictions. It will never be possible to reduce the monitoring exercise to a couple of indicators. To capture the reality of OIE standards' use, the Observatory will need to approximate the notion of implementation and adopt a multifaceted approach. This study provides directions by highlighting ways in which implementation of OIE standards takes effect, including through their uptake in domestic legislation (primary, secondary or tertiary) and their use by economic operators.

In particular, given the public nature of national legislation, uptake in domestic legislation can be tracked without confidentiality obstacles. This would nevertheless entail resources to gather the data, possibly relying on reporting / notification of relevant legislations and other regulatory measures by OIE Members and further research into the content of national legislation to determine the specific references made to OIE standards. Similar examples of legislation tracking exists in other IOs, in particular FAO Lex. Despite the challenges (Bucher, Tellechea and Mylrea, 2019[4]), the notifications of SPS measures made under the WTO requirements also provide a good start for countries to reflect on the use of OIE standards in their domestic legislation and limit their reporting efforts by satisfying both their WTO and OIE notification. That said, given the broader objectives of OIE standard-setting compared to the trade focused mandate of the WTO, there should be a reflection on whether reporting should be limited to those measures that have a significant trade impact (with the risk that the full mandate of OIE is not reflected) or extend beyond.

Monitoring the use of OIE standards by economic operators, such as importers and exporters, may be challenging in practice. For example, relevant information could be obtained through the tracking of international veterinary certificates issued by the veterinary authorities certified to assess the conformity of animals or animal products with OIE standards. However, the sharing of information is likely to be problematic due to the confidentiality of the certification details. The OIE Observatory may nevertheless be able to collect models of international veterinary certificates negotiated between trading partners to identify the use of OIE standards and then benefit from general statistics elaborated by Competent Authorities to have an overview by country of use of OIE standards by economic operators. This could help give an indication of animal health outcomes in practice.

Given the multifaceted dimensions of implementation, a core task of the Observatory could be to investigate the various forms implementation of OIE standards may take through taking stock and analysing Members' practices. This work could help the OIE refine its understanding of what constitutes good implementation of its standards and help better target the evidence and indicators to be monitored in the future.

Information sources

This report has identified the many information collection exercises that already exist in relation to OIE standards. Their key features are summarised in Table 3.3. These tools provide a key starting point for the activity of the OIE Observatory, one upon which it can progressively build to expand its activities.

Table 3.3. Overview of existing mechanisms to support and monitor implementation of OIE normative instruments

Monitoring mechanism	Current country coverage	Type of information	Frequency	Availability of information
PVS Evaluations	Mostly developing Members; ad hoc use by some developed Members	Country-level Direct references to OIE Codes	Occasionally, upon country request	Publication upon country decision
Veterinary Legislation Support Programmes	Mostly developing Members	Country-level Direct references to OIE Codes	Occasionally, upon country request	Publication upon country decision
WAHIS	All OIE Members	Country-level Few direct references to specific OIE standards	Continuously Early warning system Six-monthly and annual reports	All notified information publically available
Official Recognition of Disease Status	OIE Members with trade interest: mostly developed country and emerging economies	Country-level Direct references to OIE Codes & Manuals	Annual reconfirmation	Reports of ad hoc groups and SCAD are publically available. Applicant dossiers are not public
Self-declaration of disease status	OIE Members with trade interest: mostly developed country and emerging economies	Country-level Direct references to specific OIE Codes & Manuals	Occasionally	All information publically available
Reference Laboratories	One fifth of OIE Members; Most are developed Members	Unknown	Annual report	List of laboratories available; annual report publically available; information on data gathered by laboratories not public
Thematic items of WAD	All OIE Members	Country level and aggregates	Annual report	Aggregate results of surveys available to public through reports by expert or OIE Secretariat
OIE General Survey on Use of Anti-microbial agents	All OIE Members	Country level and aggregates	Annual report	Aggregate results of surveys available to public through reports by expert or OIE Secretariat

Monitoring mechanism	Current country coverage	Type of information	Frequency	Availability of information
Country Self-assessment on AMR action plan	All OIE Members	Few direct references to specific OIE standards	Every two years	All information publically available
Focal point seminars	All OIE Members	Diverse	Multi-annual cycle	Information mostly gathered for internal purposes; In some cases, aggregate results of surveys available to public through reports by expert or OIE Secretariat
Regional Conferences	All OIE Members	Country level and aggregates	Every two years	Aggregate results of surveys available to public through reports by expert or OIE Secretariat
WTO notifications, STCs and TPRM	All WTO Members (majority of OIE Members)	Not systematic but some references to OIE Codes & Manuals	Continuously	All information available
EU country profiles of EU Members	EU Member States	Not systematic but some references to OIE Codes & Manuals	Multi-annual cycle	All information available

Source: Author's own development.

Beyond the inherent limitations of standards covered, the information collected through existing internal OIE mechanisms pursue specific objectives, which largely differ from those of the Observatory. For example, WAHIS was set up as a mechanism to provide transparency on animal health disease status throughout OIE Members. The primary objective is therefore not to show a relation to a specific OIE standard. In the same way, the PVS Pathway gathers information on the quality of a given Member's veterinary services and provides tailored support in improving these services. Therefore, while the different mechanisms provide information on implementation of OIE standards, there is no consistency and no comparability in the information collected. The country coverage is patchy and the frequency of information not regular.

To capitalise on the existing internal sources of information, the OIE Observatory will need to invest some resources in "cleaning", standardising and gathering the information into comparable datasets. This involves broadening and systematising the information gathered through existing mechanisms to ensure some comparability of information across OIE Members – a *sine qua non* condition of any aggregation exercise. It will also involve clarifying the links with specific OIE standards – to allow for a connection with their implementation. Finally, some consolidation of information in a single source would be helpful to address its current fragmentation.

As underlined in this study, other international organisations, such as the WTO and the FAO, as well as regional organisations such as the European Commission, maintain information collection processes of relevance to the OIE. Building bridges with these data collections efforts will save on costs and may usefully complement existing OIE sources. For example, the FAO national legislation database FAOLEX is already used in certain cases as an information source in the conduct of PVS reviews, and can also feed into the monitoring efforts of the OIE Observatory in areas where there is a close relation between the scope of activities of the FAO and of the OIE. Similarly, WTO notifications allow identifying national measures that are related to OIE standards. The EU monitors its Member States measures related in particular to animal health. These information sources are public and can be easily accessed. However, these mechanisms do not specify the link with the precise OIE standards concerned. Therefore, to be able to rely on these mechanisms, the OIE Observatory will need to invest resources in clarifying this link.

To obtain detailed information on implementation, the OIE relies on data actively collected by the Secretariat (e.g. on-site missions for PVS evaluations; questionnaires developed for technical items), but also by Mandatory reporting by Members (e.g. WAHIS) as well as voluntary reporting by Members (e.g. official recognition of disease status, or self-declaration of disease status). In addition, Members are likely to collect further substantive information on areas of relevance to the OIE mandate for their domestic purposes. While over reliance on self-reported data may be problematic and raise quality and comparability issues, this could provide an additional (so far still untapped) valuable source of evidence for the OIE Observatory, which is likely "reliable" and sustainable (because it satisfies domestic needs and not only the OIE's). A survey by the OIE, for example through a dedicated Technical item of the World Assembly of Delegates, may help identify relevant national mechanisms that could feed into the information collection objectives of the OIE Observatory.

Highlighting some key principles of how the Observatory will operate

Based on the core objectives and key remit of the Observatory, the OIE will need to define its main outputs, its organisation and resources, and the key principles underlying its functioning. Some comparison with existing initiatives, however different, may be helpful to identify the key points. In this perspective, Annex D provides comparative information across a number of IO monitoring initiatives, including:

- FAOLEX
- the Health Systems and Policy Monitor of the European Observatory on Health Systems and Policies
- WHO International Health Regulations Core Capacities Implementation Status
- the Implementation Review and Support System (IRSS) of the International Plant Protection Convention (IPPC)
- ILO's regular system of supervision, and
- the Universal Periodic Review of the UN Human Rights Council.

Key outputs of the Observatory

An "Observatory" goes beyond the sole practice of collecting data. It involves some consolidation of information in one location, on-site observation and transparency / publication of results. With this in mind, existing "Observatories" in other organisations deliver several types of outputs in order to fulfil their broad mandate. These may range from searchable online databases with information on national practice and/or legislation, to cross country reports on implementation by the Membership and individual country profiles. These forms of outputs are not exclusive from each other, and several IOs combine them.

Searchable online databases provide a user-friendly source of information about the monitoring of international instruments. These may take the form of thematic, national[3] or crosscutting reports to searchable databases[4] or interactive maps.[5] They may include information about legislation, or on more factual status in a given country or region. The information made available can aim to facilitate access to the relevant legislation, as is the case for FAOLEX, or provides a more detailed overview of the level of implementation, as is the case for country profiles of the WHO International Health Regulations Core Capacities Implementation Status.[6]

The OIE Secretariat already makes information available on its website on the legislation in force in Member countries and on country disease status. Indeed, the PVS and VLSP tools gather information on legislation, and WAHIS gathers information on both disease status and control measures, and official recognition of disease status, endorsement of national official control programmes as well as self-declarations of disease status provide information on legislation and practices corresponding to specific OIE standards. Transparency is important for peer learning purposes, to test data and provide opportunities to other stakeholders (including civil society, academia, business interests) to comment and confirm or bring contradicting evidence. In turn, these inputs can feed into the monitoring and allow access to different perspectives.

The OIE Observatory could build on this information to prepare country profiles of legislation enacted by Members dealing with veterinary services, as gathered through the PVS pathway and VLSP exercises, and on disease status. This same information could be searchable by theme, disease, relevant OIE Code Chapter, country or region, in a central database. The online information could include basic links towards the relevant legislation with summaries in OIE Official languages, in the same form as in FAOLEX. Other disease status-related information, such as disease outbreaks or other related policy updates could be listed in a similar way as is the case for the country profiles of the European Health System and Policy Monitor.[7] The level of detailed information on the database may be agreed upon together with Members. Members may be unwilling to have their "level" of implementation disclosed publically, as is for example the case for the WHO International Health Regulations Core Capacities Implementation Status. The OIE Observatory may therefore keep the information on the level of correspondence between national legislation and OIE standards for more analytical reports to be published in aggregates.

The analysis of the information is an essential complement to the collection of data. It allows understanding the significance of data and relating it back to the core objective of the Observatory, i.e. a better understanding of OIE standards' implementation. Such analysis is routinely done by other international organisations. For example, the IPPC IRSS issues triennial implementation review reports that summarise the situation of the implementation of the Convention and its standards. In these reports, the focus is on assessments related to the IPPC standards. The information about country practices is disclosed in aggregates. The ILO Committee on the Application of Standards issues annual reports that include a general section on trends in the implementation of international labour standards, and sections detailing information on each Members' implementation and the exchanges throughout the year between the Members and the relevant committees.

Governance model and operational modalities of the OIE Observatory

Given its remit, the OIE Observatory needs to be appropriately resourced and located strategically to support the Organisation's strategic objectives. It should benefit from strong connection with existing data collection mechanisms and be able to influence the OIE's standard-setting process. At the same time, should the Observatory's role involve some elements of "scrutiny", i.e. of assessing whether OIE standards remain fit for purpose or are adequately implemented by their constituency, this activity would be best carried out at a certain distance from those developing the standards in the first place. The location of the Observatory and its links with the various OIE bodies will depend ultimately on its core focuses and objectives.

In addition, to ensure its credibility, the OIE Observatory should be endowed with dedicated professional staff and entail close consultations with external stakeholders. The roles for and relations of the Observatory with existing OIE bodies (regional commissions, specialist commissions and the World Assembly of Delegates) need to be clarified. The allocation of responsibilities between the Observatory and OIE Members when it comes to data collection and use should be specified.

A governing body of the OIE Observatory could help align the scope and objectives of the Observatory with those of the Organisation at large. To ensure its broad and horizontal vision of the various thematic focuses and tools of the OIE, it could be located under the direct authority of the Director General. The OIE Observatory's governing body would benefit from regular contact with external stakeholders that have information on the implementation of OIE standards, both to help the OIE Secretariat in the conduct of analytical work and to gain external insights on developments happening beyond the OIE.

Several IOs rely on independent experts and academics to support them in the analytical work, either in the actual development of surveys or in the conduct of analysis of the information gathered. The IPPC for instance hires external consultants for the design and development of surveys for the IRSS, in order to ensure their technical relevance and specificity. The ILO has set up a Committee of Experts on the Application of Conventions and Recommendations, composed of 20 eminent jurists appointed by the Governing Body for a three-year term, from different geographic regions, legal systems and cultures to provide an impartial and technical evaluation of the state of application of international labour standards in ILO Member States.

IOs consult with external stakeholders periodically to set the high-level agenda. For example, the European Health Observatory has a partnership with a number of stakeholders including international organisations, national governments, decentralised authorities and academia that participate in the European Health Observatory's Steering Committee, which determines the Observatory's strategic direction and scope of activities. Given the on-going strategic partnership of the OIE with the FAO, the WHO, the Codex and the WTO, these IOs could constitute, with others, an advisory board for the Observatory.

Members have a key role to play in providing relevant data, in involving domestic stakeholders to interact with the Observatory and in using the resulting analysis. Contact points in capitals could have a key role in following closely the work of the Observatory.

Notes

[1] www.oie.int/standard-setting/overview/oie-observatory/.

[2] Resolution No. 36.

[3] www.ohchr.org/EN/HRBodies/UPR/Pages/Documentation.aspx.

[4] List of different searchable databases in the field of IP rights: https://euipo.europa.eu/ohimportal/en/web/observatory/tools-systems-and-resources
[5] www.eublockchainforum.eu/initiative-map.

[6] See WHO country profiles available at http://apps.who.int/gho/tableau-public/tpc-frame.jsp?id=1100.

[7] See country profiles accessible here www.hspm.org/countries/france25062012/countrypage.aspx.

References

Bucher, K., D. Tellechea and G. Mylrea (2019), "Safe trade of aquatic animals and aquatic animal products: exploring the use of OIE international standards for setting sanitary measures", *OIE Scientific and Technical Review*, Vol. 38/2.   [4]

OECD (2019), *The Contribution of International Organisations to a Rule-Based International System*, OECD, Paris, http://www.oecd.org/gov/regulatory-policy/IO-Rule-Based%20System.pdf.   [2]

OECD (2016), *International Regulatory Co-operation: The Role of International Organisations in Fostering Better Rules of Globalisation*, OECD Publishing, Paris, https://dx.doi.org/10.1787/9789264244047-en.   [1]

OECD/ISO (2016), *The Case of the International Organization for Standardization (ISO)*, http://www.oecd.org/gov/regulatory-policy/ISO_Full-Report.pdf (accessed on 5 June 2019).   [3]

Annex A. Summary of the results from Questionnaire Technical Item 1, 86th General Session of World Assembly of Delegates: Implementation of OIE Standards by OIE Member countries

Generally speaking, OIE countries indicate a systematic consideration of international standards. Ninety nine per cent of respondents (144 countries) indicated that international standards are considered when developing sanitary requirements in their domestic legislation. (Only one country indicated it does not consider international standards). However, this consideration is not necessarily a legal or policy requirement. Only 57 countries responded it was a legal requirement, while 87 indicated that international standards were applied by policy but not specified in the legislation (Kahn, 2018[1]). In the absence of legal requirements to adopt international standards, their consideration is not necessarily systematic.

The legislative provisions requiring consideration of international standards tend to include broad requirements to consider "relevant international standards" in general when developing domestic regulation on animal health. Additional references are also made to OIE standards as the reference for animal health standards. Explicit references to specific standards or Code chapters are not found in the legislative documents themselves provided in the survey answers and publicly available.

- The EU Animal Health Law[1] refers in its preamble to the WTO SPS Agreement, recalling the EU's rights and obligations in this respect. In particular, the Preamble states that "If international standards exist, they are required to be used as a basis for Union measures. However, the parties to the SPS Agreement have the right to set their own relevant standards, provided that such standards are based on scientific evidence."[2] In addition, the EU mirrors the SPS Agreement in considering the OIE standards as the reference standards on animal health. It highlights that "In order to reduce the risk of trade disruption, Union animal health measures should aim at an appropriate level of convergence with OIE standards."[3] In addition, the Health Law makes reference to taking into account relevant international standards for various specific obligations.[4] In these cases, however, the relevant international standards are not explicitly mentioned.

- New Zealand Biosecurity Act of 1993 (revised in 2012)[5] acknowledges that all frameworks, codes of practice, standards, requirements, or recommended practices of international or national organisations" can be incorporated by reference into a national biosecurity document (art 142 M), suggesting that the variety of OIE instruments, whether from the Codes and Manuals or other normative instruments, may be considered for incorporation. In addition, the Biosecurity act bases certain of its legal provisions on international obligations. For example, it justifies the provisions on surveillance and prevention of New Zealand's status in regard to pests and unwanted organisms on the aim of enabling "… any of New Zealand's international reporting obligations and trading requirements to be met." (art. 42). International obligations suggest however rather binding obligations, that go beyond technical standards.

- Ukraine defines "relevant international organisations" with the OIE as well as "other international organisations that develop international standards, guidelines and recommendations related to animal health and product safety". More broadly, the law includes many references to consideration of relevant international standards in the drafting of domestic provisions, for example in the definition of an adequate level of protection of the health of animals and related health of people.[6]

As voluntary standards, the OIE Members may choose to apply a higher level of protection as long as they have scientific justification for it. When trading partners experience a concern with a country's lack of use of international standards, it may raise a specific trade concern in the SPS Committee of the WTO.

A majority of OIE respondents to the 2018 survey noted that they apply a risk analysis as the basis for setting sanitary measures.[7] In addition, 41% of respondents indicated that they used the Handbook on import risk analysis for animal and animal products (Vol. I) systematically.[8]

However, 55% of OIE countries responding to the OIE 2018 survey indicated that they do not systematically provide justification to trading partners when imposing import measures that are stricter than OIE standards (Kahn, 2018, p. 3[1]).[9] This suggests that even if OIE countries have legislation in place concerning risk analysis, the conduct of such analysis is not systematically used to justify deviations from OIE standards.

Figure A A.1. How often do you use the following publications when developing sanitary measures for imported commodities?

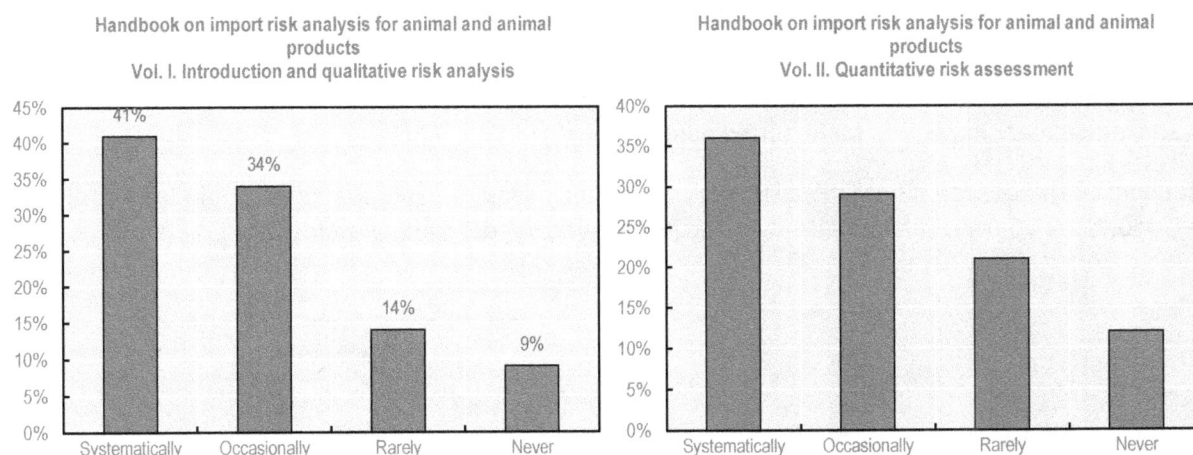

Source: OIE 2018 Survey, responses to Question 20.

Notes

[1] Regulation (EU) 2016/429 of the European Parliament and of the Council of 9 March 2016 on transmissible animal diseases and amending and repealing certain acts in the area of animal health ("Animal Health Law") available at http://eur-lex.europa.eu/legal-content/en/txt/?qid=1515592497695&uri=celex:32016r0429.

[2] Ibid. Preamble, Recital 12, of EU Animal Health Law.

[3] Ibid. Preamble, Recital 13.

[4] See for example article 1 para 2 iii); article 14 para 3; article 16 para 1 on Obligations of laboratories, facilities and others handling disease agents, vaccines and other biological products.

[5] www.legislation.govt.nz/act/public/1993/0095/latest/whole.html#dlm314623.

[6] Article 21 para 2, 4) in Ukrainian Law about Veterinary Medicine http://zakon5.rada.gov.ua/laws/show/2498-12.

[7] To question 14 of the OIE 2018 survey asking "Does your country use risk analysis as the basis for setting sanitary measures?", 59% of respondents responded Yes, required by law or other legal instrument, 34% responded yes, applied by policy but not specified in the legislation, and 7% responded no.

[8] To question 20 of the OIE 2018 survey asking "How often do you use the following publication when developing sanitary measures for imported commodities?"

[9] Responses to question 43 of OIE 2018 Survey: If import requirements are stricter than those defined in the Code, does your country provide scientific justification to your trading partners?

Annex B. Correspondence Codes and Manuals and data collection mechanisms

Terrestrial code Vol. I	Chapter 1.1.	Notification of diseases, infections and infestations, and provision of epidemiological information	WAHIS; ODS
	Chapter 1.2.	Criteria for the inclusion of diseases, infections and infestations in the OIE list	
	Chapter 1.3.	Diseases, infections and infestations listed by the OIE	
	Chapter 1.4.	Animal health surveillance	PVS; ODS; SD
	Chapter 1.5.	Surveillance for arthropod vectors of animal diseases	PVS; ODS; SD
	Chapter 1.6.	Procedures for self-declaration and for official recognition by the OIE	
	Chapter 1.7.	Application for official recognition by the OIE of free status for African horse sickness	
	Chapter 1.8.	Application for official recognition by the OIE of risk status for bovine spongiform encephalopathy	
	Chapter 1.9.	Application for official recognition by the OIE of free status for classical swine fever	
	Chapter 1.10.	Application for official recognition by the OIE of free status for contagious bovine pleuropneumonia	
	Chapter 1.11.	Application for official recognition by the OIE of free status for foot and mouth disease	
	Chapter 1.12.	Application for official recognition by the OIE of free status for peste des petits ruminants	
	SECTION 2.	**RISK ANALYSIS**	
	Chapter 2.1.	Import risk analysis	
	Chapter 2.2.	Criteria applied by the OIE for assessing the safety of commodities	
	SECTION 3.	**QUALITY OF VETERINARY SERVICES**	
	Chapter 3.1.	Veterinary Services	PVS; ODS; AMR Global Monitoring
	Chapter 3.2.	Evaluation of Veterinary Services	PVS; ODS
	Chapter 3.3.	Communication	
	Chapter 3.4.	Veterinary legislation	PVS
	SECTION 4.	**GENERAL RECOMMENDATIONS: DISEASE PREVENTION AND CONTROL**	
	Chapter 4.1.	General principles on identification and traceability of live animals	PVS; ODS
	Chapter 4.2.	Design and implementation of identification systems to achieve animal traceability	PVS; ODS
	Chapter 4.3.	Zoning and compartmentalisation	PVS; ODS
	Chapter 4.4.	Application of compartmentalisation	PVS; ODS
	Chapter 4.5.	General hygiene in semen collection and processing centres	ODS
	Chapter 4.6.	Collection and processing of bovine, small ruminant and porcine semen	ODS
	Chapter 4.7.	Collection and processing of in vivo derived embryos from livestock and equids	ODS
	Chapter 4.8.	Collection and processing of oocytes and in vitro produced embryos from livestock and horses	ODS

Chapter 4.9.	Collection and processing of micromanipulated oocytes or embryos from livestock and horses	ODS
Chapter 4.10.	Collection and processing of laboratory rodent and rabbit oocytes or embryos	
Chapter 4.11.	Somatic cell nuclear transfer in production livestock and horses	
Chapter 4.12.	Disposal of dead animals	
Chapter 4.13.	General recommendations on disinfection and disinsection	
Chapter 4.14.	Official health control of bee diseases	
Chapter 4.15.	Hygiene precautions, identification, blood sampling and vaccination	
Chapter 4.16.	High health status horse subpopulation	
Chapter 4.17.	Vaccination	
SECTION 5.	**TRADE MEASURES, IMPORT/EXPORT PROCEDURES AND VETERINARY CERTIFICATION**	
Chapter 5.1.	General obligations related to certification	
Chapter 5.2.	Certification procedures	PVS
Chapter 5.3.	OIE procedures relevant to the Agreement on the Application of Sanitary and Phytosanitary Measures of the World Trade Organization	PVS
Chapter 5.4.	Animal health measures applicable before and at departure	
Chapter 5.5.	Animal health measures applicable during transit from the place of departure in the exporting country to the place of arrival in the importing country	
Chapter 5.6.	Border posts and quarantine stations in the importing country	
Chapter 5.7.	Animal health measures applicable on arrival	
Chapter 5.8.	International transfer and laboratory containment of animal pathogenic agents	
Chapter 5.9.	Quarantine measures applicable to non-human primates	
Chapter 5.10.	Model veterinary certificates for international trade in live animals, hatching eggs and products of animal origin	PVS
Chapter 5.11.	Model veterinary certificate for international movement of dogs, cats and ferrets originating from countries considered infected with rabies	PVS
Chapter 5.12.	Model passport for international movement of competition horses	PVS
Chapter 5.13.	Model veterinary certificate for international trade in laboratory animals	
SECTION 6.	**VETERINARY PUBLIC HEALTH**	
Chapter 6.1.	Introduction to recommendations for veterinary public health	
Chapter 6.2.	The role of the Veterinary Services in food safety systems	PVS
Chapter 6.3.	Control of biological hazards of animal health and public health importance through ante- and post-mortem meat inspection	PVS
Chapter 6.4.	The control of hazards of animal health and public health importance in animal feed	
Chapter 6.5.	Biosecurity procedures in poultry production	
Chapter 6.6.	Prevention, detection and control of *Salmonella* in poultry	PVS
Chapter 6.7.	Introduction to the recommendations for controlling antimicrobial resistance	PVS
Chapter 6.8.	Harmonisation of national antimicrobial resistance surveillance and monitoring programmes	PVS
Chapter 6.9.	Monitoring of the quantities and usage patterns of antimicrobial agents used in food-producing animals	PVS; AMR General survey; AMR Global Monitoring
Chapter 6.10.	Responsible and prudent use of antimicrobial agents in veterinary medicine	PVS; AMR Global Monitoring
Chapter 6.11.	Risk analysis for antimicrobial resistance arising from the use of antimicrobial agents in animals	

	Chapter 6.12.	Zoonoses transmissible from non-human primates	
	Chapter 6.13.	Prevention and control of *Salmonella* in commercial bovine production systems	
	Chapter 6.14.	Prevention and control of *Salmonella* in commercial pig production systems	
	SECTION 7.	**ANIMAL WELFARE**	
	Chapter 7.1.	Introduction to the recommendations for animal welfare	PVS
	Chapter 7.2.	Transport of animals by sea	PVS
	Chapter 7.3.	Transport of animals by land	PVS
	Chapter 7.4.	Transport of animals by air	PVS
	Chapter 7.5.	Slaughter of animals	PVS
	Chapter 7.6.	Killing of animals for disease control purposes	PVS
	Chapter 7.7.	Stray dog population control	PVS
	Chapter 7.8.	Use of animals in research and education	PVS
	Chapter 7.9.	Animal welfare and beef cattle production systems	PVS
	Chapter 7.10.	Animal welfare and broiler chicken production systems	PVS
	Chapter 7.11.	Animal welfare and dairy cattle production systems	PVS
	Chapter 7.12.	Welfare of working equids	PVS
	Chapter 7.13.	Animal welfare and pig production systems	PVS
Terrestrial Code Vol. II	**SECTION 8.**	**MULTIPLE SPECIES**	
	Chapter 8.1.	Anthrax	
	Chapter 8.2.	Infection with Aujeszky's disease virus	
	Chapter 8.3.	Infection with bluetongue virus	
	Chapter 8.4.	Infection with Brucella abortus, B. melitensis and B. suis	
	Chapter 8.5.	Infection with Echinococcus granulosus	
	Chapter 8.6.	Infection with Echinococcus multilocularis	
	Chapter 8.7.	Infection with epizootic hemorrhagic disease virus	
	Chapter 8.8.	Infection with foot and mouth disease virus	ODS
	Chapter 8.9.	Heartwater	
	Chapter 8.10.	Japanese encephalitis	
	Chapter 8.11.	Infection with Mycobacterium tuberculosis complex	
	Chapter 8.12.	New world screwworm (Cochliomyia hominivorax) and Old world screwworm (Chrysomya bezziana)	
	Chapter 8.13.	Paratuberculosis	
	Chapter 8.14.	Infection with rabies virus	
	Chapter 8.15.	Infection with Rift Valley fever virus	
	Chapter 8.16.	Infection with rinderpest virus	
	Chapter 8.17.	Infection with Trichinella spp.	
	Chapter 8.18.	Tularemia	
	Chapter 8.19.	West Nile fever	
	SECTION 9.	**APIDAE**	
	Chapter 9.1.	Infestation of honey bees with Acarapis woodi	
	Chapter 9.2.	Infection of honey bees with Paenibacillus larvae (American foulbrood)	
	Chapter 9.3.	Infection of honey bees with Melissococcus plutonius (European foulbrood)	
	Chapter 9.4.	Infestation with Aethina tumida (Small hive beetle)	
	Chapter 9.5.	Infestation of honey bees with Tropilaelaps spp.	
	Chapter 9.6.	Infestation of honey bees with Varroa spp. (Varroosis)	
	SECTION 10.	**AVES**	
	Chapter 10.1.	Avian chlamydiosis	
	Chapter 10.2.	Avian infectious bronchitis	
	Chapter 10.3.	Avian infectious laryngotracheitis	
	Chapter 10.4.	Infection with avian influenza viruses	

Chapter 10.5.	Avian mycoplasmosis (Mycoplasma gallisepticum)	
Chapter 10.6.	Duck virus hepatitis	
Chapter 10.7.	Fowl typhoid and pullorum disease	
Chapter 10.8.	Infectious bursal disease (Gumboro disease)	
Chapter 10.9.	Infection with Newcastle disease virus	
SECTION 11.	**BOVIDAE**	
Chapter 11.1.	Bovine anaplasmosis	
Chapter 11.2.	Bovine babesiosis	
Chapter 11.3.	Bovine genital campylobacteriosis	
Chapter 11.4.	Bovine spongiform encephalopathy	ODS
Chapter 11.5.	Infection with Mycoplasma mycoides subsp. mycoides SC (Contagious bovine pleuropneumonia)	ODS
Chapter 11.6.	Enzootic bovine leukosis	
Chapter 11.7.	Haemorrhagic septicaemia (Pasteurella multocida serotypes 6:b and 6:e)	
Chapter 11.8.	Infectious bovine rhinotracheitis/ infectious pustular vulvovaginitis	
Chapter 11.9.	Infection with lumpy skin disease virus	
Chapter 11.10.	Theileriosis	
Chapter 11.11.	Trichomonosis	
SECTION 12.	**EQUIDAE**	
Chapter 12.1.	Infection with African horse sickness virus	ODS
Chapter 12.2.	Contagious equine metritis	
Chapter 12.3.	Dourine	
Chapter 12.4.	Equine encephalomyelitis (Eastern and Western)	
Chapter 12.5.	Equine infectious anaemia	
Chapter 12.6.	Infection with equine influenza virus	
Chapter 12.7.	Equine piroplasmosis	
Chapter 12.8.	Infection with equid herpesvirus-1 (Equine rhinopneumonitis)	
Chapter 12.9.	Infection with equine arteritis virus	
Chapter 12.10.	Infection with Burkholderia mallei (Glanders)	
Chapter 12.11.	Venezuelan equine encephalomyelitis	
SECTION 13.	**LEPORIDAE**	
Chapter 13.1.	Myxomatosis	
Chapter 13.2.	Rabbit haemorrhagic disease	
SECTION 14.	**CAPRINAE**	
Chapter 14.1.	Caprine arthritis/encephalitis	
Chapter 14.2.	Contagious agalactia	
Chapter 14.3.	Contagious caprine pleuropneumonia	
Chapter 14.4.	Infection with Chlamydophila abortus (Enzootic abortion of ewes, ovine chlamydiosis)	
Chapter 14.5.	Maedi-visna	
Chapter 14.6.	Ovine epididymitis(Brucella ovis)	
Chapter 14.7.	Infection with peste des petits ruminants virus	ODS
Chapter 14.8.	Scrapie	
Chapter 14.9.	Sheep pox and goat pox	
SECTION 15.	**SUIDAE**	
Chapter 15.1.	Infection with African swine fever virus	
Chapter 15.2.	Infection with classical swine fever virus	ODS
Chapter 15.3.	Infection with porcine reproductive and respiratory syndrome virus	
Chapter 15.4.	Infection with Taenia solium (Porcine cysticercosis)	
Chapter 15.5.	Transmissible gastroenteritis	

Terrestrial Manual	Part 1	General Standards	
	Section 1.1.	Introductory chapters	
	Chapter 1.1.1.	Management of veterinary diagnostic laboratories (NB: Version adopted in May 2015)	
	Chapter 1.1.2.	Collection, submission and storage of diagnostic specimens (NB: Version adopted in May 2013)	
	Chapter 1.1.3.	Transport of biological materials (NB: Version adopted in May 2018)	
	Chapter 1.1.4.	Biosafety and biosecurity: Standard for managing biological risk in the veterinary laboratory and animal facilities(NB: Version adopted in May 2015)	
	Chapter 1.1.5.	Quality management in veterinary testing laboratories (NB: Version adopted in May 2017)	
	Chapter 1.1.6.	Principles and methods of validation of diagnostic assays for infectious diseases (NB: Version adopted in May 2013)	
	Chapter 1.1.7.	Standards for high throughput sequencing, bioinformatics and computational genomics (NB: Version adopted in May 2016)	
	Chapter 1.1.8.	Principles of veterinary vaccine production (NB: Version adopted in May 2018)	
	Chapter 1.1.9.	Tests for sterility and freedom from contamination of biological materials intended for veterinary use (NB: Version adopted in May 2017)	
	Chapter 1.1.10.	Vaccine banks (NB: Version adopted in May 2016)	
	Part 2	OIE Listed Diseases and Other Diseases of Importance	
	Section 2.1.	Multiple species	
	Chapter 2.1.1.	Anthrax (NB: Version adopted in May 2018)	
	Chapter 2.1.2.	Aujeszky's disease (infection with Aujeszky's disease virus) (NB: Version adopted in May 2018)	
	Chapter 2.1.3.	Bluetongue (infection with bluetongue virus) (NB: Version adopted in May 2014)	
	Chapter 2.1.4.	Brucellosis (Brucella abortus, B. melitensis and B. suis) (infection with B. abortus, B. melitensis and B. suis) (NB: Version adopted in May 2016)	
	Chapter 2.1.5.	Crimean-Congo haemorrhagic fever (NB: Version adopted in May 2014)	
	Chapter 2.1.6.	Echinococcosis (infection with Echinococcus granulosus and with E. multilocularis) (NB: Version adopted in May 2017)	
	Chapter 2.1.7.	Epizootic haemorrhagic disease (infection with epizootic hemorrhagic disease virus) (NB: Version adopted in May 2014)	
	Chapter 2.1.8.	Foot and mouth disease (infection with foot and mouth disease virus) (NB: Version adopted in May 2017)	ODS
	Chapter 2.1.9.	Heartwater (NB: Version adopted in May 2018)	
	Chapter 2.1.10.	Japanese encephalitis (NB: Version adopted in May 2016)	
	Chapter 2.1.11.	Leishmaniosis (NB: Version adopted in May 2014)	
	Chapter 2.1.12.	Leptospirosis (NB: Version adopted in May 2014)	
	Chapter 2.1.13.	New World screwworm (Cochliomyia hominivorax) and Old World screwworm (Chrysomya bezziana) (NB: Version adopted in May 2013)	
	Chapter 2.1.14.	Nipah and Hendra virus diseases (NB: Version adopted in May 2015)	
	Chapter 2.1.15.	Paratuberculosis (Johne's disease) (NB: Version adopted in May 2014)	
	Chapter 2.1.16.	Q fever (NB: Version adopted in May 2018)	
	Chapter 2.1.17.	Rabies (infection with rabies virus and other lyssaviruses) (NB: Version adopted in May 2018)	
	Chapter 2.1.18.	Rift Valley fever (infection with Rift Valley fever virus) (NB:	

		Version adopted in May 2016)
Chapter 2.1.19.	Rinderpest (infection with rinderpest virus) (NB: Version adopted in May 2018)	
Chapter 2.1.20.	Trichinellosis (infection with Trichinella spp.) (NB: Version adopted in May 2017)	
Chapter 2.1.21.	Trypanosoma evansi infections (including surra) (NB: Version adopted in May 2012)	
Chapter 2.1.22.	Tularemia (NB: Version adopted in May 2016)	
Chapter 2.1.23.	Vesicular stomatitis (NB: Version adopted in May 2015)	
Chapter 2.1.24.	West Nile fever (NB: Version adopted in May 2018)	
Section 2.2.	**Apinae**	
	Introductory note on bee diseases (NB: Version adopted in May 2013)	
Chapter 2.2.1.	Acarapisosis of honey bees (infestation of honey bees with Acarapis woodi)	
Chapter 2.2.2.	American foulbrood of honey bees (infection of honey bees with Paenibacillus larvae) (NB: Version adopted in May 2016)	
Chapter 2.2.3.	European foulbrood of honey bees (infection of honey bees with Melissococcus plutonius) (NB: Version adopted in May 2016)	
Chapter 2.2.4.	Nosemosis of honey bees (NB: Version adopted in May 2013)	
Chapter 2.2.5.	Infestation with Aethina tumida (small hive beetle) (NB: Version adopted in May 2018)	
Chapter 2.2.6.	Infestation of honey bees with Tropilaelaps spp. (NB: Version adopted in May 2018)	
Chapter 2.2.7.	Varroosis of honey bees (infestation of honey bees with Varroa spp.)	
Section 2.3.	**Aves**	
Chapter 2.3.1.	Avian chlamydiosis (NB: Version adopted in May 2018)	
Chapter 2.3.2.	Avian infectious bronchitis (NB: Version adopted in May 2018)	
Chapter 2.3.3.	Avian infectious laryngotracheitis (NB: Version adopted in May 2014)	
Chapter 2.3.4.	Avian influenza (infection with avian influenza viruses) (NB: Version adopted in May 2015)	
Chapter 2.3.5.	Avian mycoplasmosis (Mycoplasma gallisepticum, M. synoviae)	
Chapter 2.3.6.	Avian tuberculosis (NB: Version adopted in May 2014)	
Chapter 2.3.7.	Duck virus enteritis (NB: Version adopted in May 2018)	
Chapter 2.3.8.	Duck virus hepatitis (NB: Version adopted in May 2017)	
Chapter 2.3.9.	Fowl cholera (NB: Version adopted in May 2015)	
Chapter 2.3.10.	Fowl pox (NB: Version adopted in May 2016)	
Chapter 2.3.11.	Fowl typhoid and Pullorum disease (NB: Version adopted in May 2018)	
Chapter 2.3.12.	Infectious bursal disease (Gumboro disease) (NB: Version adopted in May 2016)	
Chapter 2.3.13.	Marek's disease (NB: Version adopted in May 2017)	
Chapter 2.3.14.	Newcastle disease (infection with Newcastle disease virus) (NB: Version adopted in May 2012)	
Chapter 2.3.15.	Turkey rhinotracheitis (avian metapneumovirus) (NB: Version adopted in May 2009)	
Section 2.4.	**Bovinae**	
Chapter 2.4.1.	Bovine anaplasmosis (NB: Version adopted in May 2015)	
Chapter 2.4.2.	Bovine babesiosis (NB: Version adopted in May 2014)	
Chapter 2.4.3.	Bovine cysticercosis	
Chapter 2.4.4.	Bovine genital campylobacteriosis (NB: Version adopted in May 2017)	
Chapter 2.4.5.	Bovine spongiform encephalopathy (NB: Version adopted in	ODS

	May 2016)	
Chapter 2.4.6.	Bovine tuberculosis (NB: Version adopted in May 2009)	
Chapter 2.4.7.	Bovine viral diarrhoea (NB: Version adopted in May 2015)	
Chapter 2.4.8.	Contagious bovine pleuropneumonia (infection with Mycoplasma mycoides subsp. mycoides SC) (NB: Version adopted in May 2014)	ODS
Chapter 2.4.9.	Dermatophilosis	
Chapter 2.4.10.	Enzootic bovine leukosis (NB: Version adopted in May 2018)	
Chapter 2.4.11.	Haemorrhagic septicaemia (NB: Version adopted in May 2012)	
Chapter 2.4.12.	Infectious bovine rhinotracheitis/infectious pustular vulvovaginitis (NB: Version adopted in May 2017)	
Chapter 2.4.13.	Lumpy skin disease (NB: Version adopted in May 2017)	
Chapter 2.4.14.	Malignant catarrhal fever (NB: Version adopted in May 2018)	
Chapter 2.4.15.	Theileriosis (NB: Version adopted in May 2018)	
Chapter 2.4.16.	Trichomonosis (NB: Version adopted in May 2018)	
Chapter 2.4.17.	Animal trypanosomoses (including tsetse-transmitted, but excluding surra and dourine) (NB: Version adopted in May 2018)	
Section 2.5.	**Equidae**	
Chapter 2.5.1.	African horse sickness (infection with African horse sickness virus) (NB: Version adopted in May 2017)	ODS
Chapter 2.5.2.	Contagious equine metritis (NB: Version adopted in May 2018)	
Chapter 2.5.3.	Dourine (NB: Version adopted in May 2013)	
Chapter 2.5.4.	Epizootic lymphangitis (NB: Version adopted in May 2018)	
Chapter 2.5.5.	Equine encephalomyelitis (Eastern and Western) (NB: Version adopted in May 2013)	
Chapter 2.5.6.	Equine infectious anaemia (NB: Version adopted in May 2013)	
Chapter 2.5.7.	Equine influenza (infection with equine influenza virus) (NB: Version adopted in May 2016)	
Chapter 2.5.8.	Equine piroplasmosis (NB: Version adopted in May 2014)	
Chapter 2.5.9.	Equine rhinopneumonitis (infection with equid herpesvirus-1 and -4) (NB: Version adopted in May 2017)	
Chapter 2.5.10.	Equine viral arteritis (infection with equine arteritis virus) (NB: Version adopted in May 2013)	ODS
Chapter 2.5.11.	Glanders and melioidosis (NB: Version adopted in May 2018)	
Chapter 2.5.12.	Venezuelan equine encephalomyelitis (NB: Version adopted in May 2013)	
Section 2.6.	**Leporidae**	
Chapter 2.6.1.	Myxomatosis (NB: Version adopted in May 2014)	
Chapter 2.6.2.	Rabbit haemorrhagic disease (NB: Version adopted in May 2016)	
Section 2.7.	**Caprinae**	
Chapter 2.7.1.	Border disease (NB: Version adopted in May 2017)	
Chapter 2.7.2/3	Caprine arthritis/encephalitis and Maedi-visna (NB: Version adopted in May 2017)	
Chapter 2.7.4.	Contagious agalactia (NB: Version adopted in May 2018)	
Chapter 2.7.5.	Contagious caprine pleuropneumonia (NB: Version adopted in May 2014)	
Chapter 2.7.6.	Enzootic abortion of ewes (ovine chlamydiosis) (infection with Chlamydia abortus) (NB: Version adopted in May 2018)	
Chapter 2.7.7.	Nairobi sheep disease	
Chapter 2.7.8.	Ovine epididymitis (Brucella ovis) (NB: Version adopted in May 2015)	
Chapter 2.7.9.	Ovine pulmonary adenocarcinoma (adenomatosis) (NB: Version adopted in May 2014)	
Chapter 2.7.10	Peste des petits ruminants (infection with peste des petits ruminants virus) (NB: Version adopted in May 2013)	

Chapter 2.7.11.	Salmonellosis (S. abortusovis)	
Chapter 2.7.12.	Scrapie (NB: Version adopted in May 2016)	
Chapter 2.7.13.	Sheep pox and goat pox (NB: Version adopted in May 2017)	
Section 2.8.	**Suidae**	
Chapter 2.8.1.	African swine fever (NB: Version adopted in May 2012)	
Chapter 2.8.2.	Atrophic rhinitis of swine (NB: Version adopted in May 2018)	
Chapter 2.8.3.	Classical swine fever (hog cholera) (infection with classical swine fever virus) (NB: Version adopted in May 2014)	ODS
Chapter 2.8.4.	Nipah virus encephalitis	
Chapter 2.8.5.	Porcine cysticercosis (infection with Taenia solium)	
Chapter 2.8.6.	Porcine reproductive and respiratory syndrome (NB: Version adopted in May 2015)	
Chapter 2.8.7.	Influenza A virus of swine (NB: Version adopted in May 2015)	
Chapter 2.8.8.	Swine vesicular disease (NB: Version adopted in May 2018)	
Chapter 2.8.9.	Teschovirus encephalomyelitis (NB: Version adopted in May 2017)	
Chapter 2.8.10.	Transmissible gastroenteritis	
Section 2.9.	**Other diseases**	
Chapter 2.9.1.	Bunyaviral diseases of animals (excluding Rift Valley fever and Crimean-Congo haemorrhagic fever) (NB: Version adopted in May 2014)	
Chapter 2.9.2.	Camelpox (NB: Version adopted in May 2014)	
Chapter 2.9.3.	Infection with Campylobacter jejuni and Campylobacter coli (NB: Version adopted in May 2017)	
Chapter 2.9.4.	Cryptosporidiosis (NB: Version adopted in May 2016)	
Chapter 2.9.5.	Cysticercosis (NB: Version adopted in May 2014)	
Chapter 2.9.6.	Listeria monocytogenes (NB: Version adopted in May 2014)	
Chapter 2.9.7.	Mange (NB: Version adopted in May 2013)	
Chapter 2.9.8.	Salmonellosis (NB: Version adopted in May 2016)	
Chapter 2.9.9.	Toxoplasmosis (NB: Version adopted in May 2017)	
Chapter 2.9.10.	Verocytotoxigenic Escherichia coli	
Chapter 2.9.11.	Zoonoses transmissible from non-human primates (NB: Version adopted in May 2017)	
Part 3	**Specific Recommendations**	
Chapter 3.1.	Laboratory methodologies for bacterial antimicrobial susceptibility testing (NB: Version adopted in May 2012)	
Chapter 3.2.	Biotechnology in the diagnosis of infectious diseases (NB: Version adopted in May 2012)	
Chapter 3.3.	The application of biotechnology to the development of veterinary vaccines (NB: Version adopted in May 2010)	
Chapter 3.4.	The role of official bodies in the international regulation of veterinary biologicals (NB: Version adopted in May 2018)	
Chapter 3.5.	Managing biorisk: examples of aligning risk management strategies with assessed biorisks (NB: Version adopted in May 2014)	
Section 3.6.	**Recommendations for validation of diagnostic tests**	
Chapter 3.6.1.	Development and optimisation of antibody detection assays (NB: Version adopted in May 2014)	
Chapter 3.6.2.	Development and optimisation of antigen detection assays (NB: Version adopted in May 2014)	
Chapter 3.6.3.	Development and optimisation of nucleic acid detection assays (NB: Version adopted in May 2014)	
Chapter 3.6.4.	Measurement uncertainty (NB: Version adopted in May 2014)	
Chapter 3.6.5.	Statistical approaches to validation (NB: Version adopted in May 2014)	
Chapter 3.6.6.	Selection and use of reference samples and panels (NB: Version adopted in May 2014)	

	Chapter 3.6.7.	Principles and methods for the validation of diagnostic tests for infectious diseases applicable to wildlife (NB: Version adopted in May 2014)	
	Chapter 3.6.8.	Comparability of assays after changes in a validated test method (NB: Version adopted in May 2016)	
	Section 3.7.	**Recommendations for the manufacture of vaccines**	
	Chapter 3.7.1.	Minimum requirements for the organisation and management of a vaccine manufacturing facility (NB: Version adopted in May 2016)	
	Chapter 3.7.2.	Minimum requirements for the production and quality control of vaccines (NB: Version adopted in May 2018)	
	Chapter 3.7.3.	Minimum requirements for aseptic production in vaccine manufacture (NB: Version adopted in May 2016)	
	Part 4	**OIE Reference Experts and Disease Index**	
Aquatic Code	**SECTION 1.**	**NOTIFICATION, DISEASES LISTED BY THE OIE AND SURVEILLANCE FOR AQUATIC ANIMALS**	
	Chapter 1.1.	Notification of diseases, and provision of epidemiological information	WAHIS
	Chapter 1.2.	Criteria for listing aquatic animal diseases	
	Chapter 1.3.	Diseases listed by the OIE	
	Chapter 1.4.	Aquatic animal health surveillance	PVS
	Chapter 1.5.	Criteria for listing species as susceptible to infection with a specific pathogen	
	SECTION 2.	**RISK ANALYSIS**	
	Chapter 2.1.	Import risk analysis	PVS
	SECTION 3.	QUALITY OF AQUATIC ANIMAL HEALTH SERVICES	
	Chapter 3.1.	Quality of Aquatic Animal Health Services	PVS
	Chapter 3.2.	Communication	PVS
	SECTION 4.	**DISEASE PREVENTION AND CONTROL**	
	Chapter 4.1.	Zoning and compartmentalisation	PVS
	Chapter 4.2.	Application of compartmentalisation	PVS
	Chapter 4.3.	Disinfection of aquaculture establishments and equipment	
	Chapter 4.4.	Recommendations for surface disinfection of salmonid eggs	
	Chapter 4.5.	Contingency planning	
	Chapter 4.6.	Fallowing in aquaculture	
	Chapter 4.7.	Handling, disposal and treatment of aquatic animal waste	PVS
	Chapter 4.8.	Control of pathogenic agents in aquatic animal feed	
	SECTION 5.	**TRADE MEASURES, IMPORTATION/EXPORTATION PROCEDURES AND HEALTH CERTIFICATION**	
	Chapter 5.1.	General obligations related to certification	PVS
	Chapter 5.2.	Certification procedures	PVS
	Chapter 5.3.	OIE procedures relevant to the Agreement on the Application of Sanitary and Phytosanitary Measures of the World Trade Organization	PVS
	Chapter 5.4.	Criteria to assess the safety of aquatic animal commodities	
	Chapter 5.5.	Control of aquatic animal health risks associated with transport of aquatic animals	
	Chapter 5.6.	Aquatic animal health measures applicable before and at departure	
	Chapter 5.7.	Aquatic animal health measures applicable during transit from the place of departure in the exporting country to the place of arrival in the importing country	
	Chapter 5.8.	Frontier posts in the importing country	
	Chapter 5.9.	Aquatic animal health measures applicable on arrival	
	Chapter 5.10.	Measures concerning international transport of aquatic animal pathogens and pathological material	PVS
	Chapter 5.11.	Model health certificates for international trade in live aquatic animals and products of aquatic animal origin	

SECTION 6.		**ANTIMICROBIAL USE IN AQUATIC ANIMALS**	
	Chapter 6.1.	Introduction to the recommendations for controlling antimicrobial resistance	PVS
	Chapter 6.2.	Principles for responsible and prudent use of antimicrobial agents in aquatic animals	PVS; AMR Global Monitoring
	Chapter 6.3.	Monitoring of the quantities and usage patterns of antimicrobial agents used in aquatic animals	PVS; AMR General survey; AMR Global Monitoring
	Chapter 6.4.	Development and harmonisation of national antimicrobial resistance surveillance and monitoring programmes for aquatic animals	PVS
	Chapter 6.5.	Risk analysis for antimicrobial resistance arising from the use of antimicrobial agents in aquatic animals	PVS
SECTION 7.		**WELFARE OF FARMED FISH**	
	Chapter 7.1.	Introduction to recommendations for the welfare of farmed fish	PVS
	Chapter 7.2.	Welfare of farmed fish during transport	PVS
	Chapter 7.3.	Welfare aspects of stunning and killing of farmed fish for human consumption	PVS
	Chapter 7.4.	Killing of farmed fish for disease control purposes	PVS
SECTION 8.		**DISEASES OF AMPHIBIANS**	
	Chapter 8.1.	Infection with Batrachochytrium dendrobatidis	
	Chapter 8.2.	Infection with Batrachochytrium salamandrivorans	
	Chapter 8.3.	Infection with ranavirus	
SECTION 9.		**DISEASES OF CRUSTACEANS**	
	Chapter 9.1.	Acute hepatopancreatic necrosis disease	
	Chapter 9.2.	Infection with Aphanomyces astaci (Crayfish plague)	
	Chapter 9.3.	Infection with Hepatobacter penaei (Necrotising hepatopancreatitis)	
	Chapter 9.4.	Infection with infectious hypodermal and haematopoietic necrosis virus	
	Chapter 9.5.	Infection with infectious myonecrosis virus	
	Chapter 9.6.	Infection with Macrobrachium rosenbergii nodavirus (White tail disease)	
	Chapter 9.7.	Infection with Taura syndrome virus	
	Chapter 9.8.	Infection with white spot syndrome virus	
	Chapter 9.9.	Infection witH yellow head virus genotype 1	
SECTION 10.		**DISEASES OF FISH**	
	Chapter 10.1.	Infection with epizootic haematopoietic necrosis virus	
	Chapter 10.2.	Infection with Aphanomyces invadans (Epizootic ulcerative syndrome)	
	Chapter 10.3.	Infection with Gyrodactylus salaris	
	Chapter 10.4.	Infection with infectious salmon anaemia virus	
	Chapter 10.5.	Infection with salmonid alphavirus	
	Chapter 10.6.	Infection with infectious haematopoietic necrosis virus	
	Chapter 10.7.	Infection with koi herpesvirus	
	Chapter 10.8.	Infection with red sea bream iridovirus	
	Chapter 10.9.	Infection with spring viraemia of carp virus	
	Chapter 10.10.	Infection with viral haemorrhagic septicaemia virus	
SECTION 11.		**DISEASES OF MOLLUSCS**	
	Chapter 11.1.	Infection with abalone herpesvirus	
	Chapter 11.2.	Infection with Bonamia exitiosa	
	Chapter 11.3.	Infection with Bonamia ostreae	
	Chapter 11.4.	Infection with Marteilia refringens	
	Chapter 11.5.	Infection with Perkinsus marinus	
	Chapter 11.6.	Infection with Perkinsus olseni	
	Chapter 11.7.	Infection with Xenohaliotis californiensis	

	Chapter 2.4.7.	Infection with Perkinsus olseni	
	Chapter 2.4.8.	Infection with Xenohaliotis californiensis	
	Chapter 2.4.9.	Infection with Mikrocytos mackini	
	PART 3.	**OIE EXPERTISE**	
		Reference Experts and Laboratories for diseases of aquatic animals	
		List of Collaborating Centres for diseases of aquatic animals	

Notes: The data collection mechanisms considered are the PVS, WAHIS, the Official disease status (ODS); the Self-declaration (SD), the AMR General Survey, and the AMR Global monitoring.

Annex C. WTO SPS Notification form, G/SPS/N

1.	Notifying Member: SPS1A If applicable, name of local government involved: sps1b
2.	Agency responsible: sps2a
3.	Products covered (provide tariff item number(s) as specified in national schedules deposited with the WTO; ICS numbers should be provided in addition, where applicable): sps3a
4.	Regions or countries likely to be affected, to the extent relevant or practicable: [sps4b]　　All trading partners sps4bbis [sps4abis]　Specific regions or countries: sps4a
5.	Title of the notified document: sps5a Language(s): sps5b Number of pages: sps5c sps5d
6.	Description of content: sps6a
7.	Objective and rationale: [sps7a] food safety, [sps7b] animal health, [sps7c] plant protection, [sps7d] protect humans from animal/plant pest or disease, [sps7e] protect territory from other damage from pests. sps7f
8.	Is there a relevant international standard? If so, identify the standard: [sps8a]　　Codex Alimentarius Commission *(e.g. title or serial number of Codex standard or related text)* sps8atext [sps8b]　　World Organization for Animal Health (OIE) *(e.g. Terrestrial or Aquatic Animal Health Code, chapter number)* sps8btext [sps8c]　　International Plant Protection Convention *(e.g. ISPM number)* sps8ctext [sps8d]　　None Does this proposed regulation conform to the relevant international standard? [sps8ey] Yes [sps8en] No If no, describe, whenever possible, how and why it deviates from the international standard: sps8e
9.	Other relevant documents and language(s) in which these are available: sps9asps9b
10.	Proposed date of adoption *(dd/mm/yy)*: sps10a Proposed date of publication *(dd/mm/yy)*: sps10bisa
11.	Proposed date of entry into force: [sps11c] Six months from date of publication, and/or*(dd/mm/yy)*: sps11a [sps11e]　　Trade facilitating measure sps11ebis
12.	Final date for comments: [sps12e] Sixty days from the date of circulation of the notification and/or *(dd/mm/yy)*: sps12a Agency or authority designated to handle comments: [sps12b] National Notification Authority, [sps12c] National Enquiry Point. Address, fax number and e-mail address (if available) of other body: sps12d
13.	Texts available from: [sps13a] National Notification Authority, [sps13b] National Enquiry Point. Address, fax number and e-mail address (if available) of other body:sps13c

Annex D. Examples of monitoring efforts by other international organisations

FAOLEX

Objectives / scope	Database of national legislation, policies and bilateral agreements on food, agriculture and natural resources management
Benchmark	Thematic stocktaking under the thematic scope of FAO's mandate, without a specific assessment of compliance with international obligations
Organisation	Administered by the Development Law Service (LEGN) of the FAO Legal Office with funds from the FAO Regular Programme.
Outputs	• Database of legal and policy documents drawn from more than 200 countries, territories and regional economic integration organisations. It is constantly updated, with an average of 8 000 new entries per year. • Thematic databases organised by subject matter. • Country profiles with overview of policies, legislation and international agreements
Methodology	FAO Legal office conducts the research and develops short summaries
Data availability	FAOLEX is available at: www.fao.org/faolex/en/ FAOLEX data also feed, among other data sources, into ECOLEX a portal on environmental law, jointly operated with IUCN and UNEP since 2001. FAOLEX data is also harvested by InforMEA, a portal on Multilateral Environmental Agreements led by UNEP.

Source: www.fao.org/faolex/en/.

The European Observatory on Health Systems and Policies

Objectives / scope	The European Observatory on Health Systems and Policies supports and promotes evidence-based health policy-making through analysis of the dynamics of health-care systems in Europe.
Benchmark	Comparisons between countries, and individual assessments by country against stated objectives. No systematic assessment against a common international instrument.
Organisation	• The Observatory is composed of a Steering Committee, a core management team, a staff of 13 people based in Brussels and academic hubs in London and Berlin. • It is hosted by WHO / Europe offices • It involves a partnership with IOs, national governments, decentralised authorities, and academia.
Outputs	Country dedicated webpages with health policy updates, reform logs, and "health systems in transition" profile including information on context, organisation and governance, financing, physical and human resources, provision of healthcare services, principal health reforms, and a general assessment of the health system. An engine to compare health systems across country Searchable databases to access relevant academic articles and key reports from international organisations
Methodology	Partners define the Observatory's strategic direction, activities and research priorities most relevant to policy-makers in Europe. These priorities are translated into a 5-year development plan and broken down into annual work plans. Core management team and the wider staff of the Observatory take these work plans forward by conducting the research with the help and support of extensive international networks of experts. The Observatory staff engages directly with policy-makers and experts, and works in partnership with research centres, governments and international organisations to analyse health systems and policy trends.
Data availability	The Health Systems and Policy Monitor is a platform that provides a detailed description of health systems and information on reforms and changes that are policy relevant: www.hspm.org/mainpage.aspx The Health & Financial Crisis Monitor is an evidence resource engine dedicated to monitoring the effects of the financial crisis on health and health systems: www.hfcm.eu/

Source: www.euro.who.int/en/about-us/partners/observatory.

WHO International Health Regulations Core Capacities Implementation Status

Objectives / Scope	<ul><li>to give countries technical guidance in assessing the status of their IHR implementation and the development of IHR core capacities;</li><li>to facilitate the reporting of States parties to the WHA required under the IHR; and</li><li>to provide countries and partners with information on areas where support is needed.</li></ul>
Organisation	N/A
Outputs	<ul><li>Country profiles, with information on implementation status available by theme, and with an overall score on the average value of core capacity indicators</li><li>Public data repository</li><li>Map gallery on specific themes</li><li>Annual reports compiling statistics for key health indicators, and annual progress towards achieving the Millennium Development Goals;</li><li>Analytical reports on cross-cutting topics</li></ul>
Methodology	<ul><li>Annual self-reporting through questionnaire sent to State Parties, to assess implementation status of 13 capacities.</li><li>Joint External Evaluation mission reports</li></ul>
Data availability	<ul><li>Global Health Observatory Data:www.who.int/gho/en/</li></ul>

Source: www.who.int/ihr/procedures/monitoring/en/.

Implementation Review and Support System (IRSS) – International Plant Protection Convention (IPPC)

Objectives / scope	<ul><li>Identifying contracting parties' challenges and best practices for implementation of the International Plant Protection Convention (IPPC) and the International Standards for Phytosanitary Measures (ISPMs).</li></ul>
Benchmark	<ul><li>IPPC and ISPMs (voluntary)</li></ul>
Organisation	<ul><li>Implementation and Capacity Development Committee (IC) of the IPPC; IC Sub-group for the IRSS</li><li>Financial support from European Commission</li></ul>
Outputs	<ul><li>Triennial Implementation Review Report that summarises the situation of the implementation of the Convention and its standards. It involves two components: Implementation Review & Implementation Support.</li><li>Thematic 'desk' studies</li></ul>
Methodology	<ul><li>The IRSS is implemented on a three-year cycle. A new questionnaire is developed by technical experts for each cycle to fit the IPPC's applicable Strategic Framework.</li><li>Desk Studies are conducted for specific purposes by Secretariat staff (e.g. Equivalence, Biosecurity approach)</li></ul>
Data availability	..

Source: www.ippc.int/fr/core-activities/implementation-review-and-support-system/.

Regular system of supervision – International Labour Organisation

Objectives / scope	ILO regularly examines the application of its instruments in member states and identifies areas where they could be better applied. If there are problems in their application, the ILO assists countries through social dialogue and technical assistance.
Benchmark	ILO Conventions and recommendations (respectively binding and non-binding)
Organisation	• Examination by two ILO bodies of reports submitted by Members and of observations sent by worker's organisations and employer's organisations: • The Committee of Experts on the Application of Conventions and Recommendations • The International Labour Conference's Tripartite Committee on the Application of Conventions and Recommendations
Outputs	• Annual Reports of entire Membership, with country-specific information • NORMLEX database allowing to search for comments submitted by supervisory bodies to ILO Member countries • Web Country profiles • Technical assistance and training
Methodology	Examination of periodic reports submitted by Member States on the measures they have taken to implement the provisions of the ratified Conventions, based on legal reporting obligations found in ILO Conventions and recommendations.
Data availability	NORMLEX: www.ilo.org/dyn/normlex/en

Source: www.ilo.org/global/standards/applying-and-promoting-international-labour-standards/lang--en/index.htm.

Universal Periodic Review – UN Human Rights Council

Objectives / scope	Reviews of the human rights records of all UN Member States. The ultimate goal is to improve the human rights situation in all countries and address human rights violations.
Benchmark	(1) the UN Charter; (2) the Universal Declaration of Human Rights; (3) human rights instruments to which the State is party (human rights treaties ratified by the State concerned); (4) voluntary pledges and commitments made by the State (e.g. national human rights policies and/or programmes implemented); and, (5) applicable international humanitarian law.
Organisation	Reviews are conducted by the UPR Working Group, which consists of the 47 members of the UN Human Rights Council. Each State review is assisted by groups of three States, known as "troikas", who serve as rapporteurs. NGOs can submit information, which can be added to the "other stakeholders" report considered during the review. The submissions of stakeholders are strongly encouraged in written form, specifically tailored for the UPR, with credible and reliable information on the State under review, A voluntary trust fund was established to support the participation of developing Members in the period reviews.
Outputs	• National reports in successive "review cycles", i.e. different phases of implementation. • Country profiles online, with information collected by UN and stakeholders.
Methodology	Documents on which the reviews build on are: 1) information provided by the State under review, which can take the form of a "national report"; 2) information contained in the reports of independent human rights experts and groups, known as the Special Procedures, human rights treaty bodies, and other UN entities; information from other stakeholders, including national human rights institutions and non-governmental organizations. The evidence is discussed in UPR WG meetings. Troikas issue questions. The reports are adopted in UN Human Rights Council in plenary session. The OHCHR Secretariat compiles UN information on the state under review and prepares a summary of information received from stakeholders.
Data availability	National reports: www.ohchr.org/EN/HRBodies/UPR/Pages/Documentation.aspx Mid Term reviews posted by States on a voluntary basis: www.ohchr.org/EN/HRBodies/UPR/Pages/UPRImplementation.aspx

Source: www.ohchr.org/en/hrbodies/upr/pages/uprmain.aspx; http://ap.ohchr.org/documents/e/hrc/p_s/a_hrc_prst_8_1.pdf.

www.ingramcontent.com/pod-product-compliance
Lightning Source LLC
Chambersburg PA
CBHW080620270326
41928CB00016B/3136